To Julie
It was [?]
meet [you?],
Bon appétit
[signature]

dedication

With love to the greatest guy in the whole world, my wonderful husband, Dave. You've always been there for me and I still feel badly about the time I found you barefoot in the middle of the pointed plastic carpet grabbers, when I accidently turned your office chair mat upside down.

Copyright © 2009 Jill Lundberg

All Rights reserved.

ISBN: 1-4392-6411-2
EAN: 13: 978-1-4392-6411-9

Email any questions regarding our recipes to **lettucehelps@gmail.com**

table of contents

Breakfast in Bed 1

Quiche Me 17

Naughty, Saucy 25

Hot Nuts 35

Skinny Dipping 39

Soak Me, Stroke Me 45

Foreplay 47

Lettuce Dress You 79

Nooners 107

A Fare to Remember 117
    Wild Chicks 119
    In the Boeuf 135
    Hook it and Cook it 145
    Ménage à Trois 155
    Lotsapastabilities 165

A Little Something On the Side 169

Afternoon Delight 187

Let's See Some Cheesecake 193

Yummy Nummies 201

Happy Endings 209

Confessions of a High Price Caterer 230-233

Index 234-236

Acknowledgements 237

About the Author and the Illustrator 237

breakfast in bed

Apple Coffee Cake

Preheat oven to 350 degrees

3 Granny Smith apples, medium size, peeled and sliced very thin
5 Tablespoons sugar
1 Tablespoon cinnamon

Mix above ingredients and let stand while you beat the following
2 cups sugar
4 eggs
Dash salt

To sugar and egg mixture add
3 cups sifted flour (sift flour before you measure)
1 teaspoon baking powder
1 teaspoon baking soda
1 cup oil
1 teaspoon vanilla
¼ cup orange juice
1 cup sour cream

Beat on low until mostly blended, but do not overbeat. In greased and floured tube pan, alternately layer batter and apples.

Bake at 350 degrees for 1 hour and 10 minutes.

Cool before removing from pan. With a sharp knife, loosen the edges. Place a plate over the top of the tube pan, and invert.

A man dies. His wife brings his Urn home after the funeral. She sits down at the kitchen table and turns the Urn upside down, leaving his pile of ashes on the table.

"Herb" she says "Do you remember that pink Cadillac I always wanted? Well Herb, I drove it to the Synagogue." and she goes on "Herb, do you remember the mink coat I always wanted?

Well Herb, it was freezing today and I wore it to the services and Herb, do you remember the blow job you always wanted phew!!!   (Blowing the ashes off the table)

Apple Muffins

Preheat oven to 325 degrees
Use muffin tin liners
Yields 20 regular-size muffins or 45 mini-muffins

In a small bowl, place
1 ½ cups packed lightly brown sugar

In a separate bowl, mix together
1 cup sour or buttermilk (2 tablespoons vinegar + 14 tablespoons milk = 1 cup sour milk)
⅔ cup oil
1 egg
1 teaspoon salt
1 teaspoon baking soda
1 teaspoon vanilla

In a small bowl
Place 2½ cups flour in a small bowl. Make a well and add ½ milk mixture, and ½ of the sugar, to flour, stirring after each addition.

Fold in
Fold in diced Granny Smith apples and chopped walnuts.

Spoon mixture into paper-lined muffin tins.

Sugar Topping
Mix ⅓ cup sugar and 1 tablespoon melted butter. Sprinkle on top of muffins.
Bake at 325 degrees for 30 to 35 minutes for regular-size muffins. Bake at 325 degrees for 20 minutes for mini muffins

A man comes home very late one night. His wife demands to know where he has been.

"I had a $100 dollar bill tattooed on my penis" he explains. "That's ridiculous" she says "why would you want to do that?"

"Well" he says "I like to hold onto my money. I like to watch my money grow and the next time I want to blow $100 bucks, I know where to come."

Belgium Waffles

Makes 5 waffles

1 egg yolk
1 cup sour cream
½ cup milk
3 Tablespoons butter, melted
1 cup flour
2 teaspoons sugar
1 teaspoon baking powder
½ teaspoon salt
¼ teaspoon baking soda
1 egg white, stiffly beaten
Pam

Toppings
Strawberries, berries, ice cream, whipped cream, maple syrup, powdered sugar (see Crepes "BREAKFAST IN BED")

Preheat waffle maker. Mix all ingredients, except egg white, in a large bowl. Beat on low until moistened, then increase speed to medium and beat until batter is smooth. Do not over mix.

Beat egg white until stiff. Fold egg white into batter, by hand.

Grease hot griddle with Pam. Pour ½ cup of batter over hot griddle and cook until lightly browned, about 2 ½ minutes. Continue process until all batter is used up.

Serve immediately with toppings.

Two blondes are talking. One asks the other "Which do you think is closer, Florida or the moon"?
"That's easy" says the other "the moon"!
"Why do you say that" asks the blonde friend?
"DUH, you can see the moon!!!"

Black Bottom Muffins

Preheat oven to 350 degrees
Yields 1½ dozen muffins or
4 dozen mini-muffins

Chocolate Chip Mix
8 ounces cream cheese, softened
1 egg
⅓ cup sugar
⅛ teaspoon salt
1 cup semi-sweet chocolate chips

Beat first 4 ingredients until blended. Stir in 1 cup semi-sweet chocolate chips. Set aside. (Use mini-chocolate chips for mini-muffins.)

Dry
1½ cups flour
1 cup sugar
¼ cups cocoa
½ teaspoon salt
1 teaspoon baking soda

Liquid
1 cup water
⅓ cup vegetable oil
1 Tablespoon white vinegar
1 teaspoon vanilla
Muffin tin liners

Mix dry and liquid ingredients separately. Make a well in center of dry ingredients and fill with liquid. Stir until mostly blended. Don't over-mix.

Fill cupcake lined muffin tin ¾ full, and then add a heaping tablespoon of cream cheese/chocolate chip mixture into the center of the cupcakes.

Bake at 350 degrees for 35-40 minutes for regular muffins.
Bake at 325 degrees for 20 minutes for mini muffins.

Carrot Cake and Muffins

Preheat oven to 350 degrees
1 9x12 cake,
3 dozen muffins
10 dozen mini muffins

2 cups sugar
1½ cups oil
3 eggs
2 teaspoons vanilla

2¼ cups flour, sifted
2 teaspoons cinnamon
2 teaspoons baking soda
Nutmeg
2 teaspoons baking powder
1 teaspoon salt

2 cups shredded baby carrots
2 cups coconut
1 cup crushed pineapple, drained
1 cup walnuts, chopped
Muffin tin liners

Combine sugar, oil, eggs, and vanilla. Mix well.

In another bowl, combine flour, cinnamon, and baking soda, salt, baking powder and nutmeg. Create a well in flour mixture and pour wet mixture into it. Fold in carrots, pineapple, nuts and coconut. Mix by hand.

Bake at 350 degrees –15-20 minutes in lined mini-muffins bake 30 -35 minutes for regular muffins, 50 minutes in 9"x12" greased and floured baking pan.

Carrot Cake Frosting
8 ounces cream cheese
1½ cups butter
1 teaspoon vanilla
1 box powdered sugar (4 cups), sift if lumpy
Whole pecans, carrot curls, and green decorating tube.

Beat cream cheese, butter. Add vanilla and sugar. Spread on top of cake and decorate with pecans, carrot curls, and green icing.

Crepe Batter

Make 24 hours ahead, if possible

1 cup flour
3 eggs, well beaten
½ teaspoon salt
1½ cups milk
Vegetable oil for frying

Beat in blender or food processor and refrigerate for at least 2 hours so that the flour can expand.

Select a fry pan or crepe pan the desired size of finished crepe. Heat frying pan hot on medium heat. Pan is ready when drops of oil sizzle. Use 1 tablespoon oil for each pancake. Spread oil over pan. Pour out excess oil.

Pour in enough batter and swirl to thinly coat bottom of hot pan, Lift edges with spatula. When underneath side is lightly browned, flip the pancake. Shake a few seconds to avoid sticking. When underneath side is lightly browned, turn onto plate.

Make crepes ahead and refrigerate several days. To freeze, place parchment paper between crepes and create crepe stacks. Wrap crepe package in saran wrap. Place in freezer bags. Defrost in microwave. Do not use wax paper as wax will come off on the crepe.

Note-- for sweeter crepes, add ½ cup sugar, and 1 teaspoon vanilla.

Bellini's - sees "FOREPLAY"
Dessert Crepes - see" HAPPY ENDINGS"
Holiday Crepes - see "HAPPY ENDINGS"
Breakfast Crepes - see" BREAKFAST IN BED"

What did the egg say to the pot of boiling water? "It may take me a little longer to get hard; I just got laid by that chick over there."

Éclair Almond Coffee Cake

Preheat oven to 350 degrees
Yield 2 coffee cakes

Place parchment paper on top of cookie sheet sprayed with Pam. With pencil, draw 2 rectangles, 12" by 3", allowing space in between.

½ cup butter
1 cup flour
2 teaspoons water

Combine ingredients in a food processor (or cut butter into flour and add water). Form into a ball, divide in half. Pat each half on to the 12" x 3" forms. Set aside.

Filling
Pinch of salt
½ cup butter
1 teaspoon almond extract
1 cup flour
3½ eggs
1 cup water

Boil butter and water in heavy saucepan. Add extract. Add flour and salt all at once. Beat with electric mixer. Then add 3½ eggs, one at a time, and beat after each egg. Add extract. Divide in half and spread on dough rectangles

Bake 1 hour at 350 degrees. Remove from oven. When cool, glaze.

Glaze
1½ cups confectioners' sugar
2 Tablespoons butter, softened
1½ teaspoon vanilla
1 to 2 tablespoons water
7 ounces sliced almonds

Mix glaze and spread on top of cooled coffee cake. Sprinkle almonds on top.

To freeze, wrap in parchment paper and re-heat in parchment paper or defrost and serve without heating.

Egg and Sausage Casserole

Preheat oven to 350 degree
Make 24 hours ahead

6 eggs
2 cups milk
2 slices bread, diced (no crust)
1 teaspoon salt
½ pound sliced fresh mushrooms (canned mushrooms may be used)
1 teaspoon dry mustard
1 pound sausage links
1 cup grated sharp cheese
2 Tablespoons butter

Sauté mushrooms in butter till moisture evaporates. Set aside. Add sausage, brown and drain. Beat eggs and add milk, salt, and mustard.

In glass buttered baking dish place bread cubes, sausage, and mushrooms. Add egg mixture and top with cheese. Cover and refrigerate overnight.

When ready to serve, bake at 350 degrees for 45 minutes. Serve immediately.

A man purchases a coal mine at a very good price. He puts an ad in a local paper, looking for people to help him run the mine. After interviewing a lot of people, he hires a big strong Swede to handle the pick, a German to organize things, and a Chinaman to handle the supplies. The next day the owner arrives to see every body doing their job. The Swede is swinging the pick and the German has his clip board and if efficiently giving out assignments, but the Chinaman is no where to be found. So the owner goes looking for him. As he walks around the property, the Chinaman jumps from behind a tree and yells "SURPLIZE"!!!

Eggs Benedict

Serves 4

4 Thomas's English Muffins, fork split
8 eggs, poached
16 slices Canadian bacon
Butter
1 recipe Hollandaise sauce (see "NAUGHTY SAUCY")

Make Hollandaise and set aside. Toast English muffins and butter top side. Add two slices of warm Canadian bacon to each side topped with poached eggs (see "Helps") and cover with hollandaise. Serve immediately.

Eggs Benedict Ala Roma

Serves 4

4 petite filets
4 poached eggs
English muffins, toasted and buttered, or grilled focaccia bread
Butter
Salt, pepper, and Worcestershire sauce
Hollandaise (see "NAUGHTY SAUCY") divided into two parts)
    Add basil pesto to ½ the hollandaise and sun dried tomatoes
    to the other ½ Hollandaise sauce

In heavy fry pan, sear filets in hot butter, seasoning them with salt, pepper, and Worcestershire sauce on the seared side. Cook until desired inside temperature. Remove to side

Toast English muffins, or grill focaccia bread and scrape butter drippings from steak fry pan onto the bread. Top with filets and cover with flavored Hollandaise or Béarnaise sauce (see" NAUGHTY SAUCY")

What's the difference between a blow job and eggs benedict?

Answer: they are both something you like, but you just don't get it very often.

Elegant Fruit Torte

Preheat Oven to 350 degrees

Cream
1 cup sugar
½ cup butter (1 stick)

Crust
1 cup flour, sifted
1 teaspoon baking powder
1 egg yolk
⅛ teaspoons salt
Pam

Mix flour, baking powder, salt, and egg. Add to creamed sugar and butter and mix together by hand. Spray Pam on an 8x8 baking pan.

Filling
⅔ to ¾ cup sugar (depending on how sweet the fruit is)
Cinnamon, to taste
Lemon juice (spray)
Vanilla ice cream or sweetened whipped cream
2 pounds fresh plums, pitted and sliced (or peeled and sliced
    peaches, nectarines, apples or berries)

Slice pitted plums and spray with a little lemon juice. Place sugar and cinnamon in a baggie, add fruit slices and shake to coat. Arrange fruit over crust adding a little extra flour or corn starch if fruit appears too juicy.

Bake for 1 hour at 350 degrees. Serve with whipped cream or ice cream, warm.

***Note*--** Individual soufflé dishes can be used for single portions or double recipe and bake in a spring form for easy serving.

**Why are New Yorker's depressed?
Because the light at the end of the tunnel is New Jersey!**

Heart-Healthy Breakfast Casserole

Preheat oven to 350 degrees
Serves 6 to 8

6 slices whole wheat bread
Butter flavored Pam
½ pound ground turkey sausage
Salt
1 medium red or green sweet pepper, chopped (about ¾ cup)
½ cup chopped fresh mushrooms
1 cup shredded reduced-fat sharp cheddar cheese, divided
1 (10 ¾ ounce) can reduced-sodium condensed cream of
   Mushroom soup
1 (8 ounce) carton frozen egg product (1 cup), thawed
1 cup evaporated skim milk
¾ teaspoon dry mustard
⅛ teaspoons pepper

Cut bread into cubes; place in large, shallow pan. Bake in a 350 degree oven for 8 to 10 minutes, or until toasted, stirring once.
Spray a 12 x 7½ x 2 inch baking dish with Pam. Place half of the bread cubes in the baking dish; set aside.

Salt the bottom of a large skillet. Add sausage and sauté over medium heat. Remove and drain sausage on paper towels. Add sweet peppers and mushrooms to fat and sauté. Remove vegetables from fat and spoon mixture on top of bread cubes in baking dish. Sprinkle with half of the shredded cheese and top with remaining bread cubes.

In a medium mixing bowl, stir soup, defrosted egg, evaporated milk, mustard, and pepper. Pour over bread, pressing down cubes with the back of a spoon, moistening all the bread. Cover and chill for at least 2 to 24 hours.

To serve, bake in a 350 degree oven for 30 minutes or until a knife inserted near the center comes out clean and warm. Sprinkle with remaining cheese.

Bake for 2 to 3 minutes more. Let stand for 5 to 10 minutes before serving.

Overnight French Toast

1 loaf French bread
4 eggs
½ cup milk
¼ teaspoon baking powder
1 teaspoon vanilla
1 Tablespoon butter (or more) for pan
Maple syrup with walnuts, heated in microwave

Slice bread in ¾ inch slices. Place on 4-sided cookie sheet.

Whisk milk with eggs and vanilla. Pour over bread, turning to coat.

Let sit at room temperature for 2 hours, or refrigerate overnight.

Using an electric frying pan, melt butter. Add bread slices and brown at medium heat. When well browned, flip and brown other side.

***Note*--** sprinkle bread with toasted coconut as you sauté, or top with fresh fruit to cooked French toast and bake.

A woman dies and goes to heaven. She is greeted by St. Peter who escorts her around heaven.
All of a sudden she hears a blood curdling scream.
She asks St. Peter "What was that?"
St. Peter replies "Oh, they must be drilling holes for someone's halo"
The woman is a little disconcerted. As they continue their tour, she hears another one of those screams followed immediately by another horrible scream.
Now the woman is very disturbed and asks St. Peter for an explanation.
He says" Oh, they are drilling holes for the wings".
The woman is skeptical and says "maybe I should consider going below?"
St. Peter quickly counters with "Oh No! You don't' want to go below. They rape and sodomize the women, and she replies "But at least I have the holes for it"!!!

Sour Cream Coffee Cake

Preheat oven to 350 degrees

Sour cream
1 cup

In a separate bowl
½ cup shortening, Crisco solid
¾ cup sugar
1 teaspoon vanilla
3 eggs

Cream above ingredients with electric mixer

In a separate bowl
2 cups flour
1 teaspoon baking powder
1 teaspoon baking soda

Sift above ingredients and make a well in the center of the flour
Alternately add 1 cup sour cream and creamed mixture to flour mixture. Mix well after each addition.

In a separate bowl
6 Tablespoons butter, softened
1 cup brown sugar
2 teaspoons cinnamon
1 cup chopped nuts

Mix above ingredients.

In a greased and floured tube pan, layer ½ the batter and top with chunks of sugar nut mixture. Repeat twice, ending with a sugar layer.

Bake at 350 degrees for 50 minutes. Cool for 10 minutes and remove from pan.

***Note*--** for easier removal from tube pan, cut a piece of parchment paper to fit the bottom pf pan, removing the center of the paper, so that it will fit the bottom. Grease bottom, before pouring in the batter.

Zucchini Bread

Preheat oven to 350 degrees

3 Tablespoons butter
3 eggs
1¼ cups oil
1½ cup sugar
2 cups unpeeled raw zucchini – grated
2 cups flour
2 teaspoons baking soda
1 teaspoon baking powder
1 teaspoon salt
1 teaspoon cinnamon
1 teaspoon cloves
1 cup chopped walnuts

Beat butter, eggs, oil, sugar and vanilla until light and fluffy. Fold in grated zucchini. Sift dry ingredients together. Stir into zucchini mixture until blended. Add walnuts. Pour into floured and greased loaf pan.

Bake for 1 hour and 15 minutes at 350 degrees. Allow to rest a few minutes, then cut around the edges and remove from the pan. To freeze, wrap in plastic wrap, foil, and freeze.

Banana Bread

Preheat oven to 350 degrees

8 Tablespoons butter, softened
¾ cup sugar (may increase up to 1 ½ cups for sweeter taste)
2 eggs
1 cup flour
1 teaspoon baking soda
½ teaspoon salt
1 cup whole wheat flour
3 large extremely ripe bananas, mashed (1 cup)
1 teaspoon vanilla
½ cup walnuts or pecans, chopped

Cream butter and sugar; add eggs, one at a time, beating well. Sift dry ingredients together and add to creamed mixture. Pour into greased and floured loaf pans. Bake 60 minutes at 350 degrees.

Suggestion- Frost with chocolate icing and top with dried banana chips.

A man and his wife are playing golf, when his wife's errant tee shot goes through the window of the biggest and most expensive house on the course. Well, that is going to cost us some real money" explodes the husband. The two ride off to explain to the house owner and accept financial responsibility. As they approach the front door, they can see broken glass all over. They ring the bell and a very pleasant voice tells them to come inside.
"You must be the people who just broke my window."
The husband apologizes and explains that his wife is a terrible golfer and accepts all financial responsibility for any damages they have caused. The man starts to laugh, and says: "You actually did me a big favor. Do you see that broken blue glass? Well I was a Genie in that bottle for millions of years and you have just released me. As you know, you get three wishes. Since I have been in the bottle for so very long, I was wondering if you would give me the 3rd wish." This seemed fair to the young couple. The husband immediately said "I would like all the money in the world and never to have to work again"!! The Genie snaps his fingers and said "Done. Not only will you have all the money in the world, but you will also live a long, happy and healthy life." The woman quickly says "I would like a big Mansion in every major City in the world, beautifully decorated, with gorgeous clothes hanging in every closet". The Genie snaps his fingers and says "Done and you will never have a robbery or a fire. You will live happily and safely". The husband says to the Genie "And what is your wish"? "I would like to go upstairs and have sex with your wife. It has been such a long time. I lived in that bottle for a million years". The wife is horrified, but the husband says "You know honey, he is giving us such a wonderful life. If you are willing, I really would not mind." So she and the Genie go upstairs. After several hours of love making, the Genie turns to the wife and asks "How old is your husband?" "36" says the wife. "And how old are you?" asks the Genie.
"I am 34" replies the woman.
"And you still believe in Genies?????" he asks.

quiche me

Asparagus and Seafood Quiche

Preheat oven to 450 degrees
Reduce oven temperature to 350 degrees
Serves 6 to 8

Unbaked pastry shell
6 to 8 asparagus spears (about ¾ pound)
2 Tablespoons butter
¼ cup finely chopped shallots
½ cup pound cooked crabmeat (pasteurized, suggest Costco), or
    shrimp, cooked, peeled, deveined, and cut into small pieces)
Pinch of pepper (white, if available)
¼ cup chopped parsley
1 cup grated Swiss cheese
4 eggs
1 ⅓ cups half-and-half
½ teaspoon salt
1 teaspoon Dijon mustard
¼ teaspoon paprika

Snap off tough ends of asparagus spears. To keep asparagus green, add a pinch of baking soda to boiling, salted water. Steam asparagus until barely crisp, but tender. Rinse under cold water, drain and refrigerate.

In a medium frying pan, melt butter and cook shallots until soft, but do not brown. Remove from heat and lightly mix in crab or shrimp, pepper, and parsley. Distribute shellfish mixture evenly in pastry shell.

Beat eggs with half-and-half, salt, mustard, and paprika; and pour over seafood. Arrange asparagus spears like wheel spokes, on top of quiche and sprinkle with cheese.

Bake quiche for 10 minutes, then reduce oven temperature to 350 degrees and continue baking until crust is well browned and filling is set in center (about 20 to 25 minutes longer). If edges of pie crust start to get too dark, cover them with foil, until quiche is done, but remove before serving. Remove quiche from oven and allow standing, about 3 to 5 minutes, before cutting into wedges and serving.

Basic Quiche Batter

1½ cups custard fills a 10 inch quiche
Or 16 2 inch tarts

3 eggs, well beaten
½ teaspoon salt
1 ½ cups heavy cream
2 Tablespoons butter, melted and cooled
Dash of cayenne pepper
⅛ teaspoon nutmeg

Place all ingredients in blender and beat until smooth. Cover and refrigerate two hours or more.

Use prepared pie shell or make your own pie crust. Fill shell with your choice of cooked ingredients and pour quiche batter over ingredients, until shell is filled to the top. Bake, as for any quiche. Dough may be rolled and cut to fit any sized container. Custard cups make great individual quiches, especially for lunches for brunches, as it allows you to make assorted fillings to please all tastes. Mini muffin tins work well for appetizers.

To test if quiche is done, first feel custard with your fingers and see if it feels firm. If custard has set, and quiche appears done, place a sharp knife through center of quiche and feel if tip of knife is warm and comes out clean.

Quiche needs to sit for 3 to 5 minutes before cutting, and may be served hot or at room temperature.

Quiches may be partially baked, until custard is set. Remove from the oven, cool, freezer wrap, and freeze until ready to use. Mini quiches freeze well in freezer bags. When ready to use, remove from freezer wrap but do not defrost before baking. Bake until warmed through.

Favorite Quiche Fillings
Equal amounts of unpeeled apples, sliced and crumbled blue cheese or gorgonzola cheese, or colored pepper strips, and thinly sliced sweet onions, sautéed in butter, or steamed broccoli florets, grated cheddar cheese and butter sautéed mushrooms, or smoked salmon and fresh dill, chopped, or see recipes for crab, shrimp, vegetables, Loraine, asparagus, green chilies, and smoked pork in this chapter.

Crab Meat Quiche

Preheat oven to 500 degrees
Reduce temperature to 400 degrees
Serves 6 to 8

Pastry
1 cup flour, sifted
½ teaspoon salt
⅓ cup Crisco or butter
2-3 Tablespoons ice water
½ cup parmesan cheese, grated

Add salt to sifted four and sift again. Using dough blade and food processor, add shortening and 2 tablespoons of cold water. Process until dough forms a ball, adding more water, as needed. Wrap in plastic wrap and chill in refrigerator for 30 minutes.

Roll out ¼ of dough ⅛" thick, leaving the rest of the dough in the refrigerator. Using a cookie cutter or top of a glass, cut dough into a circle 1" larger than the diameter of mini muffin tins or desired pie plate, and fit rounds into mini muffin tins or pie plate. Repeat, until all the dough has been used up. After you cut dough rounds, take remaining dough and refrigerate, continuing to cut rounds, until all the dough has been used. If using pie plate, trim edge about ½" above top of pan. Flute with fingers to make a standing rim. Brush with lightly beaten egg white. Place in freezer for 1 hour or more. Spread parmesan cheese on top of frozen pastry.

Filling
1 ½ cup lump blue crab, pasteurized or canned (buy at Costco)
1 small onion, finely chopped
2 Tablespoons dry sherry
2 Tablespoons minced parsley
½ teaspoon salt and ⅛ teaspoon pepper
Pinch cayenne and paprika
⅛ teaspoon tarragon
4 eggs, beaten
2 cup cream

Combine crabmeat with onion, sherry, parsley, salt, pepper, cayenne, and tarragon; and spread on top of cheese. Beat eggs lightly with cream and pour over crabmeat. Sprinkle with paprika.
Bake at 500 degrees, for 10 minutes. Reduce oven temperature to 400 degrees and bake for an additional 50 minutes, until custard is set and quiche is browned on top. Use knife to test if done.

Individual Shrimp Quiches

Preheat oven to 425 degrees
Reduce oven temperature to 375 degrees
Yield 2 to 3 dozen

½ cup (1 stick) butter, at room temperature
4 ounce cream cheese, at room temperature
2 Tablespoons heavy cream
1¼ cup flour
½ teaspoon salt
2 cups roughly cut cooked, shelled and deveined shrimp
3 eggs, lightly beaten
¼ cup finely grated Gruyere or Swiss cheese
1 teaspoon freshly snipped dill weed
⅓ cup grated parmesan cheese
1½ cup heavy cream
Pam

In food processor, cream together butter and cream cheese. Add cream, flour, and salt and pulse until dough forms a ball. Wrap in wax paper and refrigerate 2 hours or overnight.

Preheat oven to 425 degrees. Roll out ¼ of pastry between two sheets of plastic wrap to ⅛" thickness. Refrigerate for a few minutes, while you roll out the rest of the pastry. Remove 1 section of rolled dough, leaving the other sections refrigerated. Using a cookie cutter or round top of a glass, cut pastry rounds that will encase mini muffin tins. Fit pastry rounds into mini muffin tins heavily sprayed with Pam. Repeat until all dough is used.

Distribute shrimp in pastry cases. Combine cream, eggs, gruyere or Swiss cheese, salt, pepper and dill. Spoon the mixture over shrimp. Sprinkle parmesan cheese on top of tarts and bake 5 minutes at 425 degrees. Reduce oven temperature to 350 degrees and bake an additional 15 minutes or until quiches are set and lightly browned on top. Cool on rack. Freeze. For same day serving, continue to bake until tops have browned. Using sharp knife, or grapefruit knife, loosen sides and remove from tins.

If frozen, remove from freezer ½ hour before serving. Preheat oven to 375. Bake 15 minutes to 20 minutes, or until warm.

Note-- shrimp can be replaced by other shellfish, mushrooms, chopped ham or bacon and sautéed onions. If filling is not shellfish, dill should be replaced by ⅛ teaspoon nutmeg.

Quiche Lorraine

Preheat oven to 450 degrees
Reduce oven temperature to 350 degrees
Serves 6 to 8

Pastry
1¼ cups sifted flour
½ cup softened butter
1 egg yolk
1 teaspoon salt
½ teaspoon dry mustard
1 teaspoon paprika
1 Tablespoon ice water

Put all ingredients in food processor with dough blade. Process until dough forms a ball. Wrap in plastic wrap and .chill in refrigerator for 30 minutes. When ready to roll, place between two sheets of waxed paper and roll to fit pie plate.
Note-- any prepared pie crust may be substituted for pastry. Follow package directions for baked pies

For 6-ounce mini quiches – spray muffin tins with Pam. Make small balls of dough and spread into muffin tin. Brush lightly with beaten egg white and freeze for 1 hour or more. For 9 or 10" pie, follow same directions or use frozen shell

Quiche Filling
1 Tablespoon butter
2 small white onions, finely chopped
½ cup shredded cooked ham
1 cup grated Swiss cheese
4 eggs
2 cups heavy cream
½ teaspoon salt
½ teaspoon cayenne (cut in half for mini quiches)
½ teaspoon white pepper (or black)
¼ teaspoon nutmeg
Note-- For tarts, cut filling recipe in half.

Melt butter in a small fry pan, and sauté onions until transparent. Place ham on bottom of pie crust. Sprinkle cheese and onion on top of ham. Beat eggs, cream and seasonings, in a blender or with beaters. Pour over onion-cheese mixture.

Serving Day
Bake on lower shelf at 450 degrees for 15 minutes. Reduce heat to 350 degrees and bake for 50 minutes on upper shelf or until custard is set.

To test if done, insert a knife 1" from edge, if it comes out clean, the quiche is done.

Mini Quiches bake at 425 degrees for 5 minutes, then 350 degrees for 10 to 15 minutes. Use 2X crust = 1X filling for mini quiches. DO NOT DEFROST before reheating.

To serve quiches without freezing, bake at 350 degrees for 25 minutes. Reduce baking time for mini quiches and bake until custard is set.

Chile Verde Quiche

Preheat oven 400 degrees
Then reduce oven temperature to 350 degrees
Yields 50 squares

18 ounce can of diced green chilies, drained
12 large eggs, beaten
Dash of salt
1½ lbs. Monterey Jack cheese, shredded
1 teaspoon baking powder
1 pint cottage cheese
1 stick prepared pie crust

Press prepared pie crust evenly across the bottom of a 4 sided jelly roll pan. Bake for 10-15 minutes at 400 degrees. Remove pan from oven and reduce oven temperature to 350 degrees.

In a small bowl, combine beaten eggs, salt, grated Monterey Jack cheese, baking powder, and cottage cheese. Spread mixture evenly over baked pie crust. Return to oven and bake for 20-25 minutes, or until knife inserted in the middle of the quiche, comes out clean. Remove from oven and allow quiche to sit for 3 to 5 minutes. Cut into small squares and serve.

Note-- quiche may be prepared in a pie plates, instead of a jelly roll pan, and served in wedges, but the yield will be less.

Smoked Pork and Spinach Pie

Preheat oven to 375 degrees
Serves 10 to 12

1 package smoked pork chops (about 4 small chops), cubed
1 Tablespoon olive oil
2 medium onions, chopped
10 ounce frozen chopped spinach
1½ cup parmesan cheese
2 cups ricotta cheese
Salt and pepper, to taste
4 eggs, lightly beaten
1 egg white, beaten
2 baked pie shells (for 1 spinach filling mixture)

Bake pie crusts according to package directions. Set aside.

Filling
Heat oil in skillet; add onion and sauté until translucent, but not browned. Microwave spinach and drain well, squeezing between sheets of paper towels. Add spinach to onion and sauté. Place mixture into a bowl and add parmesan, ricotta cheese, salt and pepper, and eggs to mixture. Spread beaten egg white on baked pie shells. Fill with spinach mixture and distribute pork. Pie may be wrapped and frozen for a later date, or baked unfrozen,

Bake pies at 375 degrees for 45 minutes, if unfrozen. Bake about 1 hour and 15 minutes, if mostly frozen.

After many weeks of dating, a couple agrees to have sex.
As they awkwardly undress for the first time, she notices that his toes are very ugly and all curled up. He notices her starring and says "as a little boy I had "Toelio".
"That is really a shame" she says.
As he takes off his trousers, she sees his knees are all very misshapen. He sees her looking and says "as a kid I had "Neasels".
He then removes his underwear and she says "Oh NO! You've had Small Cox"!

naughty, saucy

Brown Sauce

Makes 2 ½ cups

Olive oil
½ cup finely chopped baby carrots
½ cup finely chopped celery
½ cup finely chopped onions
1 plum tomato seeded and finely chopped
1 Tablespoon tomato puree (optional)
1 bay leaf (remove before serving)
¼ cup dry Sherry or Madeira wine
1 cup veal demi glaze or 1 can beef consommé soup
½ Tablespoon corn starch (more if necessary for desired thickness)
½ Tablespoon water
Salt and pepper

Heat olive oil in a heavy sauce pan, and place over medium heat. Add onion, celery and carrots and sauté vegetables until they are soft and lightly browned, adding more olive oil if necessary. Pour off fat. Add Sherry or Madeira. Cook for 1 minute. Add veal demi glaze (or beef boullion) and heat.

Place water and corn starch in a jar. With lid on shake until mixture is smooth. Add to pan gravy, continue stirring until sauce thickens. Simmer uncovered, for 10 to 15 minutes. Correct seasonings and strain sauce, scraping material off of the bottom of the strainer into the liquid as you push the softened vegetables through. Set aside until ready to heat and serve. Sauce may be refrigerated for several days, or frozen for later use.

Bordelaise Sauce

Makes 2 ½ cups

1 cup Brown Sauce, see above
1 cup red wine
½ cup shallots, finely chopped
⅛ teaspoon thyme and ground pepper

In a saucepan, combine wine, shallots, thyme and pepper. Over high heat bring to boil and reduce by half. Lower heat, add **Brown Sauce** and simmer for 20 minutes. Correct seasonings.
***Note*--** (see **Pork Chops with Roasted Garlic Bordelaise** "MENAGE A TROIS")

Barbeque Sauce for Pork Tenderloin

1 bottle A-1 steak sauce
½ cup molasses
¼ cup Worcestershire sauce
¼ cup soy sauce
2 ounces bourbon
Rosemary
Crushed black peppercorns

In a small pan, over medium heat, sauté above ingredients and reduce by half.

Serve with baked or grilled pork tenderloin, which has been crusted with rosemary, and crushed black peppercorns. Accompany with rough mashed red skinned potatoes. (see "A LITTLE SOMETHING ON THE SIDE")

To serve as an appetizer, slice the grilled warm pork and place on buttered, toasted bread rounds. Spoon on a little barbeque sauce and top with potato rouse. (Place warm mashed and buttered potatoes in a baggie, cut a small piece off the baggie corner, and pipe potato rouse onto top of sliced pork.)

Bourbon Barbeque Sauce

Buy favorite barbeque sauce, preferably honey smoked or spicy honey smoked.
Mild black molasses
Honey
Brown sugar
1/3 cup bourbon

Mix your favorite prepared barbeque sauce with honey, light brown sugar and mild black molasses. Cover and heat in microwave until all the sugar is dissolved. Add favorite bourbon and stir well.

Stone Crab Mustard Sauce

Serves 4 and yields 1 cup

3½ teaspoons dry mustard
1 cup mayonnaise
2 teaspoons Worcestershire sauce
1 teaspoon A-1 sauce
1 ½ tablespoons light cream
⅛ teaspoon salt

Beat ingredients for 3 full minutes. Chill. Serve ¼ cup of sauce for each pound of stone crabs.

Shrimp Mustard Sauce

Make mustard sauce as for stone crab, however, substitute 1½ tablespoons sweetened condensed milk (or to taste) instead of light cream. Add a dollop of yellow mustard. Mix and serve with shrimp boiled in crab boil.

Thousand Island Dressing

2 cups mayonnaise
½ jar Heinz chili sauce
¼ cup sweet pickle relish
½ cup sweet onion, chopped

Mix all ingredients together. Mixture should be shrimp color. If necessary, add more chili sauce until desired taste and color. Use as salad dressing, or as sauce for cold shrimp, crab, avocado, and lobster.

Cocktail Sauce

1½ jar Heinz chili sauce
2 tablespoon Creamy Hot Horseradish, or to taste
1 Tablespoon lemon juice
2 Ttablespoons Worcestershire sauce
1 Tablespoon sugar
Salt and pepper to taste

Mix ingredients together and serve with cold shrimp. For Crayfish, add a small amount of ketchup to mayonnaise, instead of chili sauce, green Tabasco, and old bay seasoning to taste. Also good if you use ½ and ½ sour cream.

Custard Sauce

1½ cups scalded milk
⅛ teaspoon salt
2 egg yolks
¼ cup sugar
½ teaspoon vanilla (or rum)

To scald milk, cover and boil or microwave, until skin forms on top.

Beat eggs slightly, add sugar and salt. Stir constantly with wooden spoon while gradually adding hot milk. Add just enough hot milk to egg mixture to warm eggs, and then gradually add the remaining milk. Cook in double boiler until mixture thickens and coats a spoon.

When cool, add vanilla. Chill before serving. Mixture will thicken as it cools.

Double or triple recipe for plenty of sauce, it's the best part! Serve with Snow Pudding and Floating Island "HAPPY ENDINGS"

Crème Anglaise

8 egg yolks
1 cup sugar
1 teaspoon vanilla
3½ cups half-and-half (scalded)

In the bottom of a double boiler, beat egg yolks. Add sugar and beat until lemon yellow. Beat in scalded cream a little at a time.
To make custard, cook mixture over double boiler, until custard coats a spoon. Do not allow water in the bottom pan to boil, as this may curdle the custard.
If mixture curdles, immediately pour custard into a cold bowl and place bowl over another bowl filled with ice cubes and cold water. Beat custard, using electric beaters on high, until custard becomes smooth again.

Pour custard into individual serving dishes and top with caramelized meringue eggs islands (see **"Floating Island** and Snow Pudding "HAPPY ENDINGS")

Refrigerate until ready to serve. Lasts several days, refrigerated.

Hollandaise Sauce

Yields approximately 1 cup
4 egg yolks
½ cup butter, room temperature
Pinch of cayenne pepper
Juice of ½ lemons (remove any pits)
Salt and pepper to taste

Combine all ingredients in top of double boiler and stir to make a paste. Boil water in the bottom of the double boiler. Take out scant ¼ cup boiling water and add it to the egg/butter paste. Reduce the boiling water to barely simmering. Using either an electric mixer or an electric whisk beat the egg/paste mixture until it reaches the consistency of pudding. If sauce curdles see "Hints". Add 1/3 cup of small pieces of cooked lobster or shrimp, for a yummy taste.

Béarnaise Sauce

Make Hollandaise Sauce and add one tablespoon of frozen Mung

Mung

1 Tablespoon chopped shallots
1 Tablespoon fresh cracked pepper
⅔ cup red wine vinegar (or enough to cover mixture) divided
3 Tablespoons dried tarragon leaves

In a heavy fry pan, cook shallots, pepper, and half the red wine vinegar, or enough to cover the mixture in the pan. Simmer until liquid is mostly gone. If necessary, add more wine vinegar to prevent mixture from sticking to pan.

Add 3 tablespoons tarragon and the rest of the vinegar, adding more if necessary to cover the mixture. Boil until most of the liquid is gone, making sure there is always enough liquid so that mixture does not stick to the pan. If necessary, drain liquid.

It's best to make a larger amount and put one tablespoon in a square of saran wrap. Twist tightly. Repeat until mung is used up. Place individual "kisses" in plastic baggie and freeze. Add later to Hollandaise sauce to create Béarnaise Sauce.

Grand Marnier Fruit Sauce

Serves 8 to 10

6 egg yolks
1 pint heavy cream, whipped
1½ cups powdered sugar
2 Tablespoons Grand Marnier liqueur
Speck of lemon juice
Fresh fruit, raspberries, strawberries, black berries, nectarines, and peaches

Beat egg yolks until thick and lemon color. Add sugar and continue beating until eggs are very stiff. Stir in whipped cream, lemon juice, and Grand Marnier. Place fresh fruit in glass goblets. Top with plenty of sauce and serve.

Note-- sauce may not be made ahead, as it will separate. Should this happen, stir or beat mixture until it comes together and is thick.

A woman comes home from work to find her husband crying his eyes out.
"What's wrong" she asks?
"I just come from the Doctors", the husbands sobs
"I only have twenty-four hours to live"!!!!
"That's horrible", the wife exclaims.
"Is there anything I can do for you "?
"Would you have sex with me" the husband asks?
"Of course", the wife says.
Four hours later, he reaches over and asks "Can we have sex again, since I only have twenty hours left to live?
The wife is very sympathetic and readily agrees.
When he asks if they can have sex, yet a third time, for old time's sake, she starts to get a little annoyed.
Finally he taps her on the shoulder and says
"Honey, could we do it again? I only have four more hours to live."
She turns over and says
"Look, you don't have to get up in the morning, but I do"!!!

Sugar Free Chocolate Sauce

Sugar free Hershey chocolate candy
Milk or cream
Butter, a small pat
¼ to ½ teaspoons Vanilla

Unwrap the sugar free chocolate pieces and place in a heavy sauce pan over low heat. Add just enough milk to keep chocolate pieces from seizing. Stir constantly until melted.

Remove from heat, stir in vanilla and a pat of butter. Stir until smooth and creamy. Serve immediately, as chocolate will harden quickly.

Refrigerate to store. To reheat, add a little more milk or cream, and warm on low heat.

A man goes to a whore house. The prostitute asks him what he wants?
He says he doesn't know, what does she suggest?
She asks him how much money he has and he tells her $ 20.
"I can't do much for $ 20, "she says.
"Well can't you do anything?" the man begs.
"Well I guess I could give you a "PENGUIN" she suggests.
"I have never heard of that" says the customer.
So she takes off his belt, then she drops his trousers, she then drops his boxer shorts. She gets down on her knees and starts to give him a unbelievably fabulous blow job.
She is into it for about 40 seconds, when she suddenly stops and walks away.
The startled guy, all his clothes around his knees, his hands at his sides at a 90 degree angle, minces after her yelling "Hey, where are you going?"

Newburg Sauce

2 Tablespoons butter
3 egg yolks, beaten
¼ cup Madeira wine or Sherry
½ teaspoon paprika
1 teaspoon salt

Melt butter in a sauce pan, add wine and cook for 2 minutes
Beat egg yolks and add cream a little at a time, beating thoroughly after each addition. Stir mixture into warm sauce. Allow to thicken, stirring constantly. Serve with lobster and seafood.

Fricassee Sauce

¼ cup butter (or chicken fat)
¼ cup flour
1 ½ cups good chicken stock, warm (see **Poached Chicken** "WILD CHICKS") or use boxed rotisserie stock
½ cup cream
¼ teaspoon salt
1 teaspoon pepper
Yellow food coloring

Heat butter and add flour. Stir until smooth and bubbly. Stir in warm stock, a little at a time, eliminating any lumps that may form.
Add cream and stir until smooth. Add a few drops of food color until the sauce turns a rich creamy yellow.

To serve as Entree
Serve over cooked chicken (poached or boneless rotisserie) and accompany with white rice and a green vegetables.

Maitre D' Hotel Butter Sauce

¼ cup butter
¾ Tablespoon lemon juice (optional)
½ teaspoon salt
⅛ teaspoon pepper
½ teaspoon parsley, chopped fine

Mix above ingredients in a small bowl, working the lemon juice in slowly, as you mix with a wooded spoon. Spread over top of hot grilled steak or fish, just as grilling is finishing and before you serve.

Sweet and Sour Sauce

2 Tablespoons cornstarch
¾ cup sugar
⅓ cups rice wine vinegar
1 teaspoon dry sherry
⅓ cups water
2 Tablespoons soy sauce

Mix all ingredients in a sauce pan and boil until mixture thickens, stirring constantly. Keep refrigerated.

Wasabi Aioli

Mix powdered Wasabi with a little water to make a paste. Add mayonnaise to taste. When done, aioli should be a pale green color.

Cajun Vodka Sauce

1 cup mayonnaise
1 Tablespoon plus 1 teaspoon Vodka
2 teaspoons Chef Paul Prudhomme's Seafood Magic seasoning blends
¼ teaspoon chopped garlic
1 teaspoon chopped parsley
¼ cup plus 1 teaspoon finely chopped sweet onion

Mix ingredients together and chill for several hours. Sauce will keep for several days, if refrigerated

Note -- serve with Ahi tuna or scallops wrapped with bacon.

Sign in church bulletin "Low Self Esteem Group will meet Thursday at 7:00 P.M.

Please use back door"

hot nuts

Meringue Pecans

Preheat oven 325 degrees

1 egg white
¼ teaspoon cinnamon
¼ teaspoon salt
⅓ cup sugar
4 Tablespoons melted butter
2 cups (½ pound) pecan halves

To prepare pan, grease a shallow 10 x 15 inch jelly-roll pan, or use parchment paper.

Beat egg white until stiff. Mix cinnamon and salt into sugar. Keeping the beater running, add sugar mixture, 1 tablespoon at a time, to beaten egg white. Fold in melted butter and pecans. Spread pecan mixture in prepared pan and bake for 15 minutes in 325 degrees preheated oven.

Remove pan from oven. Using a spatula, carefully flip the pecan mixture, one small section at a time. When all the pecans have been turned over, return the pan to the oven. Bake an additional 15 minutes. Watch them carefully- do not allow them to burn! Cool pecans on paper towels.

Orange Pecans

2 cups sugar
¾ cups of milk
3 Tablespoons grated orange peel
3 Tablespoons orange juice
2 cups pecans
Parchment paper (or aluminum foil)

Combine sugar, milk, and orange peel in a saucepan. Cook until mixture forms a soft ball when dropped into a glass of cold water. Let cool for a few seconds. Add orange juice. Beat mixture until cloudy. Add pecans and continue stirring until nut coating begins to crystallize.

Pour onto parchment-lined pan. Let cool and then break nuts apart. Freeze in freezer baggies to store.

Sweet and Spicy Pecans

Preheat oven to 300 degrees
Makes 1 cup

¼ cup sugar
1 cup warm water
½ cup pecan halves

Stir together until sugar is dissolved. Add pecan halves and soak nuts for 10 minutes. Drain and discard sugar mixture.

2 Tablespoons sugar
1 Tablespoon chili powder
⅛ teaspoon cayenne pepper
Pam

Combine sugar, chili powder, and cayenne pepper. Add pecans, toss to coat and place evenly on a foil lined cookie sheet that has been Pam sprayed. Bake at 300 degrees for 10 minutes or until nuts have lightly browned, stirring once.

Four golfing buddies have a standing tee time at 8:00 every Saturday morning. One beautiful Saturday they arrive, only to find another foursome planning to tee off ahead of them. They scream at the starter that they are always the first foursome to go off the tee every Saturday morning and they demand to be the first off this Saturday. The starter tries to explain that the reason he had switched things was that the men in the other foursome were deaf and dumb and he thought it might be better if they went off first. The regulars are very stubborn and still insist on being first off the tee box. The starter gives in and the buddies tee off. As they are about to hit their second shots, a ball comes through the air and almost hits them. They turn around and look back at the tee box to see who is hitting into them. The driver on the tee box holds four fingers in the air.

Toasted Nuts

Preheat oven to 300 degrees

Pecans, walnuts, almonds, pine nuts or nuts of choice should be placed nuts, whole or chopped, on a foiled cooking sheet, and dotted with pats of butter. Bake at 300 degrees until lightly browned. Watch carefully as nuts will burn quickly. Alternative method is to place nuts in a fry pan and sauté nuts in melted butter, over low flame, or until lightly browned. When cooled, place in baggies, seal, and store in freezer until ready to use. Nuts can be reheated before using.

Toasted Almonds

Preheat oven 300 degrees

Coat almond slivers with melted butter and spread on foiled cookie sheet. Bake at 300 degrees for 20 to 30 minutes, or until lightly brown. Spread on paper towels, sprinkle with salt and set aside.
When cool, place in baggie and freeze.

Toasted Filberts and Toasted Hazelnuts

Preheat oven 300 degrees

Spread nuts in a shallow baking dish, in a single layer and coat with melted butter. Bake 10 to 12 minutes at 300 degrees. To remove skins, place warm nuts in a sealed baggie and let them stream. Remove from baggie, wrap in a towel and rub until skins come off.

A man with a hair lip enters a nut store and tells the man behind the counter that he is interested in purchasing some nuts. "How muth does a pound of cathyews cost?"
"$35 dollars a pound" responds the salesman.
"That's vewy expensive, how about your hathelnuts" asks the hair lip. "They are also $35 a pound"
"Well how about your pithsatheos" asks the frustrated hair lip. "They too, are $35 per pound.
The customer decides not to buy any nuts, but says to the proprietor" Thank you for not making fun of the way I pronounce things"
"Thank you" says the proprietor for not mentioning how long my nose is"
"Your NOSE, I thought that was your DICK, because you're nuts are so high"

skinny dipping

Fanny Farmer

5 cups mayonnaise
2½ Tablespoons lemon juice, bottled
1½ Tablespoons chopped parsley
5 Tablespoons grated onion
2½ cups heavy cream, whipped
1¼ teaspoons salt
1¼ teaspoons paprika
½ teaspoon curry powder
1 Tablespoon minced garlic

Blend ingredients. Make 24 hours ahead, if possible. Cover and refrigerate. Great for grilling, marinating, as a dip or sauce.

Use with Pita Triangles, Crab Cakes and Conch Fritters ("FOREPLAY"). Vegetables, raw or fried ,meat, seafood, and poultry

New Orleans Dip

¼ cup slivered almonds
2 strips of bacon, crumbled
1 cup grated cheddar cheese
1 teaspoon onion
½ cup mayonnaise
¼ teaspoon salt

Mix ingredients in a small bowl and serve with crackers.

Cream Cheese Bean Dip

Preheat oven to 350 degrees

1 8 ounce package cream cheese, room temperature (do not use fat-free cream cheese or mixture will not melt properly)
1 can refried beans
½ package Taco seasoning
Salsa (hot, medium, or mild)
Grated Mexican cheeses
Corn chips (white, yellow, or black)

Spread cream cheese around top and sides of oven to table baking dish. Mix ½ package of Taco seasoning mix with refried beans. Spread on top of cream cheese. Add layer of salsa and top with grated cheese.

Bake uncovered, in preheated 350 degree oven until mixture is hot and bubbly. Serve with corn chips.

Crab Mornay

½ cup butter
1 bunch small green onions, chopped
½ cup finally chopped parsley
2 Tablespoons flour
1 pint half and half cream
Cayenne pepper, to taste (start with a pinch and add as needed)
½ pound grated Swiss cheese
1 Tablespoon sherry, or to taste
½ pound to 1 pound of back fin lump crabmeat, or Alaskan King Crabmeat
Sturdy buttery crackers

Melt butter in heavy skillet and sauté onions and parsley over medium heat.

Blend in flour, cream, and cheese until cheese is melted.
Add remaining ingredients and gently fold in crabmeat.

Place crab mixture in a chafing dish. Place chafing dish over small amount of warm water, adding more as needed. Stir occasionally to prevent separation. Accompany with crackers.

Crab Dip

1 pound lump crab meat
6 ounces cream cheese, room temperature
4 ounces of sour cream
3 Tablespoons lemon juice
Worcestershire, to taste
Garlic powder, to taste
¼ cup sweet onion, very finely chopped

Blend all ingredients except crab. When smooth, carefully fold crab into mixture, being careful not to break up the lumps of crab.

Mixture may be served cold or heated in the oven at 350 degrees until tip of knife comes out hot, when plunged into dip center.

Shrimp Maria

Preheat oven to 350 degrees
Use as entrée or appetizer

2 pounds shrimp, cooked, cleaned, and deveined
2 cans artichoke hearts, not marinated, drained,
2 cups mayonnaise
1 cup parmesan cheese
1 Tablespoon lemon juice
1 Tablespoon Worcestershire sauce
2 cups unseasoned bread crumbs
½ cup butter, more as needed

Buttered Bread Crumb Topping
Melt butter in 10 inch fry pan. Add crumbs all at once, adding more butter, as needed. Cook crumbs until browned

To use as Appetizer
Use Filo fluted cups, purchased in the frozen section of the grocery store. Chop cooked shrimp and artichokes into very small pieces and fill bottom of cups. Mix together, mayonnaise, lemon juice, and Worcestershire. Sprinkle with parmesan cheese and top with buttered bread crumbs. Bake at 350 degrees until warm, about 10 minutes.

To use as Entree
Mix together, mayonnaise, cheese, lemon juice, shrimp, and Worcestershire sauce, and place in a buttered casserole. Top casserole with buttered bread crumbs and bake until warm, about 10 minutes at 350 degrees. To test doneness, stick a sharp knife through center of casserole. When you pull it out, feel the knife to see if it is hot. If used as a main course, serve over rice and accompany with a colorful vegetables.

Why do men die first?

Because they want to!

Smoked Shrimp & Artichoke Spread

Serves 4

1 8-ounce package cream cheese (room temperature)
¼ teaspoon Worcestershire sauce
1 Tablespoon fresh lemon juice
Dash of Tabasco
2 teaspoons Spike all purpose seasoning (available at health food store)
⅛ teaspoon liquid smoke
¼ (10 ounce) package frozen cooked artichoke hearts, diced
¼ pound shrimp (26 to 30 / pound), cooked, peeled, deveined, and diced
Buttered and toasted French baguette slices, or crackers

Place in food processor, cream cheese, Worcestershire, lemon juice, Tabasco, Spike and liquid smoke. Pulse mixture until smooth. Remove to serving dish and fold artichoke hearts and shrimp into the mixture. Serve with toasted French baguette.

Shrimp Dip

8 ounces cream cheese
1 stick of butter
½ cup celery
1 small chopped onion
2 teaspoons mayonnaise
2 teaspoons lemon juice
Garlic powder
Onion powder
Dash of Worcestershire
Pinch of pepper
¾ pound shrimp, cooked, cleaned, deveined, and chopped

Place all ingredients, except shrimp, into a food processor and pulse until mixture is creamy. Remove to serving dish and stir in shrimp. Serve with crackers or celery sticks.

Taco Bread Round or Salad

1½ to 2 pounds lean ground beef
1 onion, sliced
1 6 ounce can tomato sauce
1 15 ounce can tomato sauce
Salt and pepper, to taste
1 Tablespoon chili powder
½ to 1 can fire roasted green chiles (hot, medium, or mild)
3 pound bread round (white farmers round loaf)

Toppings
Finely chopped sweet onions, chopped tomatoes, cubed avocado, Mexican grated cheese, chipotle dip or sour cream, and pickled jalapeño rings.

With a sharp bread or serrated knife, slice through the top of the bread round, creating a large bread bowl. Carefully remove the top and scoop out most of the bread remaining inside the bowl, leaving a thick lining of bread especially at the bottom. You do not want the taco to leak through your bowl. Cube the removed bread and seal in a baggie until ready to serve.

Sprinkle bottom of electric fry pan with salt. When hot, add meat and onions and sauté. Drain fat and stir in rest of ingredients. Cover and simmer, stirring occasionally for 30 to 40 minutes, adding water if necessary. Fill bread round, add toppings, surround with bread cubes and corn chips and serve

Spinach Bread Round

2 packages frozen spinach, thawed and squeezed dry between paper towels
2 packages Knorr's vegetable soup mix
2 cups mayonnaise
2 cups sour cream
1 cup water chestnuts, sliced
¼ cup onion, chopped
1 two pound round bread loaf (farmers round or pumpernickel round)

Mix ingredients together 24 hours before serving, and refrigerate. Cut and carefully remove top of bread round. Scoop out bread, leaving a bread lining. Cube removed bread. Fill bread bowl with dip and place on serving platter and accompany with cubed bread.

soak me, stroke me

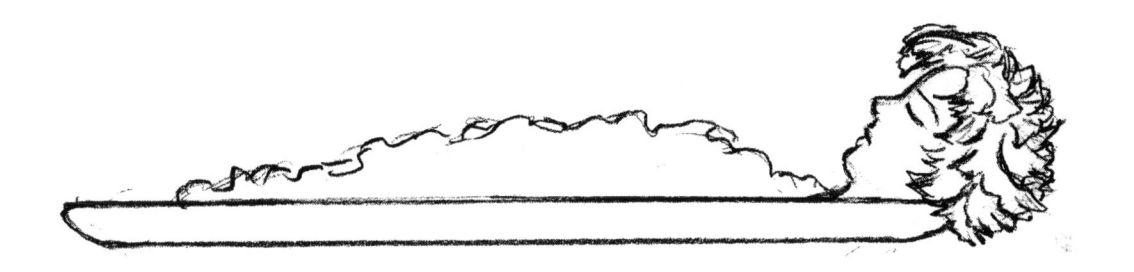

Marinade for Chicken or Pork

¾ cup salad oil
¼ cup soy sauce
2 Tablespoons lemon juice
3½ Tablespoons honey
½ Tablespoon garlic powder
½ Tablespoon ginger
1 cup scallions, chopped, including tops

Marinade for Steaks

1 cup red wine vinegar
½ cup soy sauce
½ cup olive oil

Mix together and place in a large sealable baggie. Add the steak and marinate meat for no longer than 3 hours. Meat may be marinated when purchased and frozen. Do not defrost the meat thoroughly before cooking.

Marinade for Tenderloin

Make 24 hours ahead

3 cups vegetable oil
1 Tablespoon garlic, crushed
1 Tablespoon salt
1 Tablespoon sugar
1 Tablespoon fresh ground pepper
¼ cup whole black peppercorns (or green)
1 cup Jack Daniels whiskey
Mushrooms, sliced
Onions, sliced

Mix above ingredients in a glass container and marinate tenderloin slices for 3 to 5 hours. Remove tenderloin and marinate mushrooms and onions in the remaining marinade.

Tenderloin slices may be pan fried in butter and oil, or grilled and topped with a pat of butter before serving.

foreplay

Ahi Tuna

Preheat electric fryer to 375 degrees

Ahi tuna, sushi grade
Sesame seeds, black and white
Tri-colored pepper blend, Lawry's
Wonton squares
Peanut oil for frying
Paprika
Wasabi paste or powder
Mayonnaise
Butter
Sesame oil
Wonton squares and paprika

Cut Ahi tuna into strips (columns), about 1½ to 2" wide. Roll tuna in black and white sesame seeds, and Lawry's tri-colored seasoned pepper blend. Crust tuna heavily on all 4 sides and freeze.

Heat butter and oil in a heavy fry pan, until very hot, and place frozen Ahi tuna columns in pan, and sauté, turning Ahi, until all four sides are heavily seared. Ahi should be crusty on the outside and rare on the inside.

***Note*--** It is easier to assure rareness, if tuna is mostly frozen before searing.

Cut wonton squares into 4 piece squares. Sprinkle with paprika to help brown quickly. Preheat electric fryer to 375 degrees. Drop wonton triangles, one at a time, into fryer basket and lower into the hot fat. Remove wontons, as they start to turn light brown and drain on paper towels. Wontons will darken quickly, as they cool.

Slice tuna columns ¼ inch thick and place on wontons. Top with **Wasabi Aioli Sauce** (see "NAUGHTY SAUCY")

To serve Ahi tuna as main entree
For dinner portion, do not cut tuna in strips; leave as one whole filet, about ½ pound per person. Follow above cooking directions. Rare tuna is best achieved by freezing toasted sesame coated filet. In a heavy fry pan, melt butter and sesame oil until hot. Sear frozen Ahi tuna over very high heat. Insides will stay rare. Serve with Wasabi Aioli Sauce (see "NAUGHTY SAUCY")

Artichoke Appetizer

Preheat oven to 350 degrees

½ cup chopped onion
½ cup water
4 well-beaten eggs
¼ cup dry bread crumbs, unseasoned
½ teaspoon salt
⅛ teaspoon pepper
⅛ teaspoon oregano
1 can mushroom pieces
2-3 drops Tabasco
2 cups grated cheddar cheese
2 6-ounce jars marinated artichokes (Cara mia), drained and chopped

In a small fry pan or microwave, cook onion in ½ cup of water, until tender, about 5 minutes.

Combine eggs, bread crumbs, salt and pepper, oregano and Tabasco. Stir in onion, cheese and artichokes.

Spray a 2-quart (11x7) Pyrex with Pam. Fill with mixture.
Bake at 350 degrees for 18 to 25 minutes, until top is slightly browned and mixture is firm.

Cut in 1" squares and serve on plain crackers or wheat thins.

To freeze- cook thoroughly as indicated. Cool and freeze. Reheat frozen, at 350 degrees, until inserted knife comes out warm.

Engravings on side by side tombstones:

HERE LIES MY WIFE "STILL COLD"

HERE LIES MY HUSBAND "STIFF AT LAST"

Bellini Crepes

Serves 8

10 crepes (see Basic Crepe recipe " BREAKFAST IN BED")
1 medium onion, sliced very thin
Butter
Caviar (preferably white fish not lumpfish, black in color)
Hard boiled egg, chopped
Sour cream

Make 8 crepes, following basic crepe recipe. This may be done several days ahead and stored in the refrigerator or freezer. Make sure that you place a piece of parchment paper between each crepe before storing for easy separation.

Melt butter in fry pan and sauté onion until lightly browned. If you wish to do this step ahead, reheat onions briefly, either by sautéing briefly again or by heating in the microwave.

In a large heavy fry pan, heat a little butter and place 1 crepe in the pan. Warm one side briefly, and turn. Place a little onion, sour cream, caviar, and chopped egg on top of ½ of the crepe. Fold empty side over top of filled side to close crepe. Add a little brandy or cognac to the pan and warm. Avert your eyes and ignite brandy flaming the crepe. Carefully remove crepe from pan to serving plate, spooning remaining brandy on top. Place a dollop of sour cream, top with additional caviar and serve.

Serve with frozen vodka shooters. (see "Help" for frozen flower encrusted vodka bottle)

Liquid Viagra called "Mydicksadud"

It's for those guys who like "A shot straight up"

Broiled Ham and Almond Stuffed Mushrooms

Preheat Broiler

Mushrooms, about 3 pounds, extra large for stuffing (Costco has the best)
5 Tablespoons butter
3 onions finely chopped
1¼ cups ham, minced (about ½ pound), not sweet
¼ teaspoon dry mustard
2 Tablespoons fresh parsley, minced
¼ cup sour cream
1 cup chopped almonds
¼ teaspoon salt
Pinch of pepper

Wash mushrooms. Remove stems and finely chop.
Melt 3 tablespoons butter in a skillet and sauté onions and chopped stems. Add the rest of the ingredients, except caps.

Brush caps all over with 2 tablespoons of melted butter. Place in broiling pan, rounded side up, and broil for 1 minute.

Remove and add some of the mushroom juice from the pan to stuffing mixture, but do not make mixture too runny. Fill the cups with stuffing. Brush with melted butter on top of the mushroom stuffed caps and broil under medium flame until warm. Do not burn. Place on platter and serve.

Mushroom Roux

Variety of assorted mushrooms, sliced
Onions, sliced very thin
Garlic, chopped
Parmesan cheese, to taste
Mayonnaise, enough to bind
Canned artichokes (not marinated)
Butter

Sauté onions and garlic in butter, until translucent, add mushrooms and artichokes and cook until roux forms. Place in food processor; add cheese and mayonnaise and puree. Serve warm with crackers.

Magnificent Mushrooms

1 pound mushrooms, wiped clean, halved, or sliced if very large
½ cup dry vermouth
½ cup olive oil
½ cup red wine vinegar
1 garlic clove, crushed
2 Tablespoons onion, chopped
1 Tablespoon basil
1 teaspoon salt and ½ teaspoon pepper
½ teaspoon sugar
½ teaspoon dry mustard

In a small bowl, mix together above ingredients except mushrooms and pour over cleaned mushrooms, allowing them to marinate for several hours or refrigerated in a sealed container, for several days.

A huge storm goes through town leaving rising water and floods. Members of the Jewish Congregation, concerned for their Rabbi, row a boat to the Synagogue.
"Rabbi," they say "get in the boat and we will row you to safety".
"No", says the Rabbi "I will be fine. The Lord will look after me"
As the water continues to rise, the Rabbi is practically drowning and he hears a helicopter above.
A voice came over the Megaphone and yells: "Rabbi, catch onto the rope ladder and we will pull you to safety."
"No" gargles the Rabbi" I must stay with the Torah. The Lord will protect me."
But the Rabbi drowns and when he meets God, he says
"God, I have been your faithful servant my whole life and I have served you well. How could you let me drown?"
A booming voice replies, "I sent a rowboat and a helicopter for you, what more do you want?"

Bruschetta

Preheat oven 350 degrees

Garlic toast rounds
Sour dough baguette, sliced thin at the bakery
Melted butter
Garlic salt

Brush both sides of bread slices with melted butter. Place on foil lined cookie sheet, in a single layer. Sprinkle with garlic salt, and bake at 400 degrees, until lightly browned on both sides, turning once if necessary. Wrap in aluminum foil until ready to use, or freeze for later use.

Topping needs to marinate for 24 hours

1¼ pounds plum tomatoes, chopped
4 cloves garlic (or 2 teaspoons jarred chopped garlic)
30 fresh basil leaves, scissor cut into small pieces
½ cup good quality olive oil
1 teaspoon salt
1 teaspoon pepper
½ to ¾ pound of whole milk mozzarella cheese, cubed (not fresh)
4 cloves of garlic (or 2 teaspoons of chopped garlic)

Marinate tomatoes, basil leaves, oil, salt, pepper, and cheese overnight and refrigerate. In the morning, stir in the garlic and continue to marinate. Just before serving, drain the tomato mixture. Place tomatoes, mozzarella cheese, garlic and basil leaves on top of the toasted garlic rounds, and place on cookie sheet single layer. Bake in 300 degree oven, until cheese is slightly warmed, but not melted, as you do not want the tomatoes to cook. Remove from oven and serve immediately. Bruschetta is also delicious if you add cooked, grilled or stir fried shrimp, to the top of the Bruschetta.

**Two blonde women are waiting at the airport for their husbands who have been gone on a golfing trip.
As the men get off the plane, the one woman says "Oh no" my husband is carrying a dozen red roses!! Now I have to spend the weekend with my legs up!!"
"What's the matter" says her friend "Don't you have a vase?"**

Chicken Pepperidge Farm Fingers

Preheat oven to 350 degrees
Makes 70 fingers

10 chicken breasts, boneless, skinless (about ½ pounds each)
24 ounces sour cream
12 ounces mayonnaise
3 tablespoon Worcestershire sauce
3 bags Pepperidge Farm seasoned stuffing
Butter, melted (1 to 2 sticks butter for each tray of chicken fingers)
Cranberry sauce (canned or fresh cranberry sauce)

Using scissors, cut chicken into bite sized pieces.

In a large bowl, mix sour cream, mayonnaise, and Worcestershire.

Place one bag of Pepperidge Farm Stuffing on a large cookie sheet, breaking up any large pieces. Dip raw chicken fingers into the mayonnaise mixture and roll in stuffing crumbs, packing the stuffing onto the chicken using the palms of your hands. You may have to do this several times, making sure the stuffing adheres to the chicken. Repeat process until all the chicken has been breaded, opening the other bags of stuffing, as needed. Stuffing will get wet, so use one bag at a time discarding stuffing as it gets too wet to use.

Foil several 4 sided cookie sheets and place breaded chicken pieces, leaving a little space between each piece. Melt butter and dribble over chicken, turning chicken so that both sides are buttered.

Bake for 20 minutes, turning each piece to allow browning on both sides. Chicken is done when the insides are not pink and the outside is crispy.

To serve as entree
Use chicken pieces that are on the bone and have skin, such as breasts, wings, thighs, and drumsticks. Follow directions for **Pepperidge Farm Chicken Fingers**. Bone in chicken pieces may be in freezer bags, frozen and use when needed. Coat with melted butter on both sides and bake for 1 hour to 1 hour and 15 minutes, or until chicken is not pink inside and is crispy on the outside. If raw chicken has been frozen, defrost slightly so butter will be absorbed into the stuffing and bake at 350 degrees until chicken is not pink inside and is crispy on the outside.

Chicken Teasers

Serves 8

24 bites sized chicken medallions, boneless and skinless
3 Tablespoons butter
1 Tablespoon olive oil
Salt, pepper, and paprika to taste
1 Tablespoon chopped garlic
24 toasted sour dough garlic bread rounds (see **Surf and Turf** "FOREPLAY")
Fanny Farmer dip (see "SKINNY DIPPING")

Marinate raw chicken fingers in a baggie filled with Fanny Farmer dip, for several hours.

Melt butter and oil in a heavy fry pan and when hot, add chicken pieces, leaving plenty of room between pieces. Season with salt, pepper, and paprika, and sauté until chicken is tender and white in the center. Add garlic and sauté the last minute of cooking, being careful not to let the garlic burn.

Top each bread round with a piece of chicken, spoon on remaining garlic butter evenly over the chicken croutons. Add a dollop of Fanny Farmer and serve immediately.

**A wife comes down to breakfast only to find her husband reading the paper and ignoring her.
She bangs her fist on the table and declares "I am going out to get a job"
He laughs and says "Oh yeah, what work do you think you can do?"
She replies "The only thing I know how to do".
At lunch time she returns and plunks down $ 50.50 on the table.
The husband asks "Who paid you 50 cents"?
"Everybody" she replies!**

Coconut Fried Shrimp

Preheat electric fryer to 375 degrees

2 pounds raw shrimp (21 to 25 to the pound)
Coconut, flaked
Beer batter (see "A LITTLE SOMETHING ON THE SIDE")
Flour
Oil for frying
Sweet and Sour Sauce, Piña Colada Sauce, or Cocktail Sauce (see "NAUGHTY SAUCY")

Heat oil to 375 degrees in an electric fryer.

Peel shrimp and remove black vein. Dip peeled shrimp into baggie filled with flour. Shake off excess flour and dip shrimp into beer batter. Roll battered shrimp into coconut and place into fryer basket. Fry until golden brown, adding shrimp one at a time to basket. Remove and drain on paper towel. Serve immediately with Sweet and Sour Sauce, Pina Colada Sauce, or Cocktail Sauce.

To serve Coconut Fried Shrimp as entree
Allow ½ pound shrimp per person, and follow the directions above.

Conch Fritters

Preheat fryer to 350
Makes 50

2 cups self-rising flour
2 cups cleaned and chopped conch (buy it this way)
1 large onion, diced
1 green pepper, diced
Salt & pepper
2 dashes Tabasco
2 eggs, slightly beaten
Garlic powder
Cayenne pepper
Jalapenos
Milk

Combine all above ingredients. Add enough milk for fritters to hold their shape. Form into fritters and fry at 350 degrees in corn oil and bacon fat. Drain on paper.

Serve immediately with cocktail sauce, Thousand Island dressing, Cajun vodka sauce, or Fanny Farmer. Note- may be made ahead and frozen, then either baked or refried to heat

A woman comes down to breakfast one day and her husband says "Honey, I am really sorry, but we have no money and you're going to have to go out on the street and sell your body".
"Oh no" she says. "If there was only some other way".
He says "But there is not, however, I am going with you to make sure nothing happens to you."
She goes in to change her clothes.
He drops her on Main Street and says he will be parked just around the corner.
For the first hour no one even comes by. Finally a sailor approached her and asks her how much she charges for her services.
She says "Wait a minute" and goes down the street and knocks on the car window.
Her husband rolls down the window.
She asks "How much should I charge?"
"$ 100 bucks" he says.
So she goes back to the sailor and tells him the amount. He says "I only have $ 20 bucks. Will you do a blow job for $ 20 bucks?"
She says "Wait a minute" and she goes back to her husband's car and knocks on the window.
He rolls down the window.
"He only has $ 20 bucks, can I do a blow job for that?" she asks?
Her husband says "Okay".
So she goes back down the street and tells the sailor that she can do it for the $20.
They go down a nearby alley and the sailor undoes his belt buckle, pulls down his pants and out comes the most gorgeous penis she had ever seen.
"Wait a minute" she says and runs down the street to her husband's car.
She knocks on the window, and he rolls it down.
"Can I borrow $80 bucks" says the wife?

Corn and Black Bean Quesadilla

Preheat oven to 350 degrees
Serves 4

3 large flour burritos
1 red onion (Bermuda), sliced thin
1 can small black beans
Grated Mexican cheeses
Cayenne pepper
Paprika
Olive oil
Sour cream
Fresh ripe Hass avocado (soft to the touch without feeling air)

Cut avocado in half, so that you create two boats. Scoop out avocado, leaving the shell intact. Mash avocado and add salt and pepper to taste, and a little onion very finely chopped. (Finely chopped tomatoes and tabasco sauce are also options) Mound mashed avocado around avocado pit, cover tightly with plastic wrap and refrigerate until ready to use.

Foil a cookie sheet and place one flour burrito on the foil. Brush with olive oil, sprinkle with cayenne pepper, and spread one layer of beans, sliced red onion, and top with plenty of grated cheese. Brush both sides of the next burrito with oil and place on top of cheese. Repeat above process of cayenne, beans and cheese. Brush both sides of last burrito with olive oil and place on top of cheese layer. Sprinkle top with paprika (not cayenne) and bake in preheated 350 degree oven until cheese is melted. Remove from oven and cut into pie wedges using a pizza cutter.

Fill 1 avocado shell with sour cream and the other shell with the mashed avocado mixture. Accompany wedges with fresh salsa and avocado and sour cream boats.

Jewish Cowgirl Song to the tune of "Bonanza"
Get it out
Get it up
Get it in
Don't mess my hair up!!!

Crispy Shrimp Fried in Wontons

Makes 44 to 50 shrimp
Preheat electric fryer to 375 degrees
Serves 8

2 pounds shrimp, 21 to 25 per pound, raw, peeled, and deveined
1 package square wontons cut on diagonal to form triangles
Peanut or vegetable oil, for frying

Wrap wonton around, covering shrimp. Glue ends together with a drop of water.

Fill electric fryer to correct level and heat to 375 degrees. Place shrimp covered wontons, in fry basket, leaving plenty of room between shrimp and fry until crispy. Remove and drain on paper towels. Do not cook too many shrimp at one time, as it will be hard to maintain the proper frying temperature. Serve with Asian Dipping Sauce (see below)
Note-- to serve as entrée, allow ½ pound of shrimp per person.

Asian Dipping Sauce

Makes approximately ¾ cup

2 bunches of cilantro, leaves only (or 1 bunch parsley and 1 bunch cilantro)
1 teaspoon soy sauce
1 Tablespoon plus 1 teaspoon brown sugar
1 Tablespoon rice wine vinegar
2 teaspoons fresh ginger, grated
2 Tablespoons sesame oil
2 teaspoons vegetable oil
Garlic (optional)

Place all ingredients, *except sesame oil and vegetable oil*, in food processor, and pulse. With food processor running, add oils in a steady stream. Process until thickened (should have consistency of creamed spinach).

Make at least 24 hours ahead. Store in refrigerator.

Elegant Crab

Serves 4 to 8

1 pound back fin super lump crab meat (suggest Phillips or Blue Star found at Costco)
Fresh cut long stem flowers, or wild flowers
Thousand Island dressing (see "NAUGHTY SAUCY")
Cocktail sauce (see "NAUGHTY SAUCY")

Place crab meat in a glass or silver container. Place on large silver tray. Place pink dressing and cocktail sauce in separate containers and place beside crab meat. Arrange long stem fresh flowers attractively on the tray. Crab may be accompanied with fans of avocado slices that have been sprayed with lemon juice to keep from turning brown,

Note-- crab may be replaced with cooked shrimp or in addition to the crabmeat. Crab claws may also be used.

Crab in Fluted Filo Cups

Preheat oven to package directions
Serves 15

1 package frozen fluted Filo cups (found at local grocers)
1 pound back fin lump crabmeat (Phillips, Blue Star, or Chicken of The Sea, found at Costco)
Bacon, cooked
Avocado, peeled
Lemon juice
Thousand Island dressing (see "NAUGHTY SAUCY")

Bake Filo cups according to package directions. Fill cups with crab, bacon pieces, lemon sprayed avocado sticks, and top with a dollop of Thousand Island dressing.

Note-- cooked shrimp, cut into small pieces, may be substituted for crabmeat. If available, spay Filo cups with apricot spray to keep Filo from getting soggy.

Fried Lobster

Preheat electric fryer to 375 degrees
Serves 8 to 12 as appetizer
Serves 2 to 4 entrée

4 slipper cold water lobster tails (about 1 ½ to 2 ounces each)
Oil for electric fryer
Beer batter (see "A Little Something on the Side")
Sweet and sour sauce (see "Naughty Saucy")
Flour

Cut through the back of the lobster tail with a scissors. Split the underneath side as well. Using your fingers, remove the lobster from the shell. If lobsters are frozen, defrost slightly before removing the lobster. Split the tail open lengthwise, and remove meat. Dip the lobster meat, first in flour, shaking off excess, and then in the beer batter. Preheat oil to 375 degrees. It is a lot easier to use a fryer with a basket. Lower the fryer basket into the hot fat. Drop the battered lobster pieces, one at a time, into the basket. Do not fry too many lobster pieces at one time, as you want the fat to remain at 375 degrees, while frying. If necessary, fry the lobsters in small batches. When the pieces are golden brown (you can sprinkle the lobster meat with a little paprika after they have been dipped in the beer batter, if you want them to brown quickly). When browned and the lobster is cooked through, remove and drain on paper towels. Cut the finished lobster strips into bite sized pieces.
Serve with sweet and sour sauce.

To serve Fried Lobster as Main Course or First Course

When loosening the lobster from the shell, leave one end of the lobster attached to the shell and the other end loose (like a tongue). Follow the above directions, frying the lobster, shell and all.
Serve with sweet and sour sauce (see "NAUGHTY SAUCY") or purchase bottled sweet and sour sauce found in ethnic isle of grocery store) As a first course, or luncheon, allow one tail per person. You will need more, probably two per person, if served as a main course.

Sign in Bar:
Beer Nuts: $ 1.00   Deer Nuts: under a buck

Grilled Artichoke

Preheat grill

Artichokes
Pinch of baking soda
1 Tablespoon of vinegar or lemon juice
1 teaspoon salt
Balsamic vinaigrette dressing (see "LETTUCE DRESS YOU" Granny Apple Salad)
Fanny Farmer sauce (see "NAUGHTY SAUCY")

Fill large pot with water 1/3 full. Add salt, baking soda, and 1 tablespoon vinegar or lemon juice, cover and bring to a rapid boil.

Add artichokes, cover and boil or steam (in steamer basket), until leaves pull out easily and are tender. Drain and cool until you can handle them comfortably. If you wish to do this several days ahead, tightly wrap the drained artichoke in plastic and refrigerate and refrigerate. When ready to use, heat grill.

When you are ready to serve, split the artichokes in half. Place halves on a cookie sheet, cut side up. Spoon on balsamic vinaigrette, and allow to soak in.

Spray hot grill with Pam, being careful to have grill top up and eyes averted. Place cut side down on hot grill (leaves are up). If the artichokes are cold, you may need to close the grill lid briefly, until artichokes are completely warm. Serve with Fanny Farmer sauce.

Note -- also excellent as side vegetable with main entrée.

An old Gal in a nursing home gets the hots for a guy down the hall. Every night she would go to his room and give him a hand job.
One night she saw another old woman go into his room. She watches as the other woman replaces her.
Furious, she rushes into his room the very next morning and demands to know what this new woman has that she doesn't have.
"PARKINSONS" yells the man.

Grilled Shrimp in Pea Pods

Heat grill
Preheat oven to 300

2 pounds extra large shrimp, raw, cleaned and deveined (21-25)
2 cups cilantro leaves (remove from stems)
2 Tablespoon garlic, chopped
2 teaspoons paprika
1 teaspoon salt,
½ cup olive oil
¼ teaspoon cayenne pepper
¼ cup lemon juice
Peapods
Cream Cheese
Toasted pine nuts
Pineapple apricot horseradish

To toast pine nuts
Line a cookie sheet with foil and spread pine nuts evenly over surface. Dot nuts with butter and bake at 300 degrees, until lightly toasted. Watch carefully as nuts will burn quickly.
Pine nuts may also be sautéed in a little butter, to brown

Marinade
Pulse cilantro leaves (no stems), garlic, paprika, salt, and oil in food processor. Remove to bowl, cover shrimp and marinate 15 minutes. Before grilling, add lemon juice.

Boil water with salt and a pinch of baking powder. Add peapods and blanche peapods quickly and immediately drain and rinse with cold water to stop the cooking. Refrigerate until cool. Cut string edges of peapods, with scissors and carefully open. Spread with cream cheese and pineapple apricot horseradish, and toasted pine nuts. If you cannot find apricot pineapple horseradish, you can make it by combining apricot preserves, pineapple preserves, and horseradish to taste.

Heat grill. Place marinated shrimp in grill basket and grill till firm, turning once, about 2 minutes on each side. Place 1 shrimp on each prepared peapod and serve.

Note-- for an easier appetizer, place blanched pea pods on a serving platter with apricot horseradish, cream cheese, pine nuts, and let every one help themselves, eliminating the shrimp.

Maryland Crab Cakes

Makes 60 crab cake appetizers

1¼ cups mayonnaise
3 whole eggs
2 Tablespoons Coleman's dry mustard
1 Tablespoon Worcestershire sauce
3 pounds lump crabmeat (Costco Philips, Blue Star or Chicken of the Sea)
1 scant cup unseasoned bread crumbs
½ cup yellow pepper, very finely diced
½ cup red pepper, very finely diced
Butter
Oil

Mix together first four ingredients (may be done well ahead and refrigerated) When ready to use, gently add crab, being careful not to break up lumps. Add breadcrumbs and diced peppers. If mixture seems too moist, add enough bread crumbs so that mixture will hold together when medallions are formed. If you need to make more appetizers, you can increase the amount of bread crumbs.

In heavy pan or electric frying pan, add just enough butter and oil to grease pan. Form silver dollar-sized crab cakes medallions. Sauté until brown on both sides, adding more butter and oil as needed.

Cajun Vodka Sauce (see "NAUGHTY SAUCY")

Crab Cakes as Main Entree

Serves 2 to 3

⅓ cup plus 4 teaspoons mayonnaise
1 egg
2 teaspoons dry mustard
1 teaspoon Worcestershire sauce
1 pound lump crabmeat (Costco Philips, Blue Star or Chicken of the Sea)
¼ cup unseasoned bread crumbs
⅓ cup red pepper, very finely diced
Butter
Oil

Follow above directions for crab cakes and top with **Cajun Vodka Sauce** (see "NAUGHTY SAUCY")

Meatballs in Beer

100 small meatballs

1½ pounds lean ground beef (or ¾ pound ground chuck
 and ¾ ground round)
2 eggs, well beaten
¾ cups milk
1 cups Italian flavored bread crumbs

Mix above ingredients together and make about 100 small meatballs. There are two ways to cook the meatballs, and either is fine. If you are making a lot, it is easiest to foil cookie sheets and bake meatballs in preheated oven to 350 degrees, and bake for 10 minutes. If you are making a small amount, meatballs may be sautéed in a large skillet with a small amount of melted butter.

Sauce
½ to 1 cups of beer
½ cups light brown sugar
1 bottle Heinz Chili sauce

Place above ingredients in a large sauce pan, stir and bring to a boil. Reduce heat to simmer and add cooked meatballs. At this point meatballs may be frozen to use at a later date. When defrosted, you may need to add more beer to thin the sauce. Heat and serve.

Every week there is a local talent show at the red neck bar in town.
One night a gay guy stands in front of the microphone. He laces his fingers together, closes his palms together and exclaims "I have a surprise in here and if anyone guesses what it is, I will have a surprise for you"
"The Empire State Building" yells out a big strapping male in the back.
"I think we have a winner!" says the gay.

Mediterranean Loaf

Long piece of French bread cut lengthwise in half. Pull out insides (save for use in stuffing)
4 tomatoes, peeled and chopped
4 green onions, chopped, including green tops
½ cup each black olives and green olives with pimentos
2 Tablespoons fresh parsley, chopped
Some capers
½ teaspoon dried mint leaves
Sprinkle of thyme
1 Tablespoon any kind of grated cheese
2 to 3 Tablespoons olive oil, to make mixture soft
Lemon juice
Salt and pepper, to taste
Insides of bread, crumbled

Mix up. Put back in bread. Put top of bread back on and secure with foil.

Refrigerate for at least 24 hours. Slice into thick pieces and serve.

A man is having an affair with a woman, when her husband arrives home unexpectedly.
"Quick" she says to her lover "stand in the corner and rub this baby oil all over your naked body".
She runs into the bathroom and grabs dusting powder. She quickly dusts him all over. The powder sticks to the oil and he is totally covered in white. She puts a tray in his hand and tells him to stand perfectly still.
"What is that in the corner" the husbands ask queasily?
"It's a statue, the Smith's bought one and I just loved it" she replies.
Her husband wakes up in the middle of the night and goes downstairs. He makes himself a sandwich and pours a glass of milk. He eats half the sandwich and drinks half the milk.
The rest he takes upstairs and puts it on the statue's tray.
He whispers "I was at the Smith's for 3 days and no one even brought me a glass of water".

Moroccan Brie Topping

Wedge of brie cheese
Chopped dates
Chopped walnuts (or chopped nuts of choice)
Honey
Crackers

In a bowl, combine nuts and dates. Add enough honey to bind ingredients. Refrigerate until ready to use.

Remove rind from top and sides of brie wedge. Top with nut mixture, add crackers and serve.

Brie with Pinot Noir Syrup

Makes about ½ cup

2 cups Pinot Noir wine
½ cup raw sugar
1 fresh rosemary sprig chopped, or teaspoon dried (optional)
1 Tablespoon balsamic vinegar
1 Tablespoon butter

In heavy fry pan, over medium heat, cook sugar until sugar liquifies and starts to turn brown. Do not stir. Turn off heat and stir in wine. Raise heat to high and cook, stirring until caramel dissolves again. Add rosemary (optional) and cook over heat until sauce is reduced and mixture is syrupy, about 10 to 15 minutes.

Place brie on serving plate. With a sharp knife, carefully remove white rind from sides and top of brie.

Place brie wedge on serving plate. Top with sauce or serve sauce on the side. Serve with crackers and decorate serving plate with fresh fruit, such as grapes (champagne grapes, if available), apple and pear slices, peeled and sprayed with lemon juice, strawberries and raspberries.

Mushroom Sherry Toast Cups

Preheat oven to 350 degrees

4 Tablespoons butter, melted
3 Tablespoons shallots, chopped
½ pound mushrooms, sliced
2 Tablespoons flour
1 cup very heavy cream (do not whip)
½ teaspoon salt
⅛ teaspoon cayenne pepper
1 Tablespoon fresh parsley (optional)
1½ Tablespoon chives
½ teaspoon lemon juice
1⅓ teaspoon (or more, to taste) cooking sherry
Freshly grated parmesan cheese

Melt butter, sauté shallots (until tender), add mushrooms. Cook until liquid is gone. Stir in flour. Cook a few minutes, soaking up all of the butter and cooking out the flour taste.

Add cream. Stir until thick and smooth and add all ingredients. Make ahead. Just before baking, fill toast cups, add freshly grated parmesan cheese to top. Bake at 350 degrees for 8 minutes.

Cups for Mushroom Sherry

Preheat oven to 400 degrees

Use a glass that will make white breads rounds sized to fit into mini muffin tins that have been heavily greased with soft butter. Palm press bread rounds to flatten bread and fit them into the tins. Bake at 400 degrees until the bottom of the round is lightly toasted. Fill toasted cups with mushroom mixture and bake. (See directions above) or place toasted cups in freezer baggies and freeze until ready to use.

Additional toast cup fillings
Back fin lump crabmeat or small cooked shrimp pieces, avocado, and Thousand Island dressing (see "NAUGHTY SAUCY")
Chicken Salad (see "LETTUCE DRESS YOU" **Exotic Chicken Salad** or **Tarragon Walnut Chicken Salad**)
Mushroom Roux (see "FOREPLAY")
Ham and Swiss cheese with ground mustard, melted in the oven.
Cooked bacon, lettuce and diced tomatoes, with mayonnaise.
Deviled Egg Salad (see "LETTUCE DRESS YOU")

Parmesan Shrimp Pillows

Preheat oven 350 degrees

White bread slices
Shrimp, cooked, cleaned, and deveined
1 cup fresh grated parmesan cheese
1 cup mayonnaise

Mix parmesan cheese and mayonnaise together.

Using a shot glass or small cookie cutter, make small, crust less rounds of bread. Top with a shrimp, and mound on mayonnaise and parmesan mixture.

Place rounds on a foiled cookie sheet and bake until warm and brown on top. To insure tops brown, broil for the last minute. Cool for a minute, and serve.

When Mrs. Finkelstein's husband of many, many years dies. All of her friends try to fix her up. Since her husband had been the only man she had ever slept with, dating was very awkward.
But one night her blind date actually works.
Conversation at dinner goes well and neither side seems to want the evening to end. He invites her back to his apartment and she eagerly accepts. One thing leads to another and he asks if she "wants to fool around"?
They go into separate rooms to undress. He returns with a giant hard-on. She is naked except for a pair of black lace thongs.
"What's with the black panties" he asks?
"I follow our religious traditions" she replies "I'm still in morning"
"You can touch me any place I am not wearing black" she says.
That was kind of a mood killer and he takes her home.
She doesn't hear from him for several weeks. The next time they go out to dinner, their evening is even better. As they are lingering over coffee, he again invites her to his apartment. This time, after undressing separately, he appears with an erect penis sheathed in a black condom.
"What's with the black condom" she asks?
"I am coming to pay my respect" he answers.

Piña Colada Shrimp

Preheat electric fryer to 375 degrees
Serves 4 to 6

1½ cup corn starch, divided
2 cups plain bread crumbs
2 cups sweetened coconut flakes
1½ cup liquid piña colada drink mix, divided
2 Tablespoons powdered sugar
⅓ cup spiced rum
1 lb. raw jumbo shrimp, peeled, deveined, butter flied
⅓ cup sour cream
⅓ cup canned crushed pineapple, drained

Place 1 cup corn starch in a bowl; set aside.

Combine bread crumbs, ½ cup corn starch, and coconut flakes in a separate bowl; set aside.

In a separate bowl, combine 2 cups piña colada drink mix, powdered sugar, and rum and set aside. Place corn starch in a baggie and coat shrimp, shaking off excess, then dip in piña colada mixture, then in coconut mixture, then back into piña colada mixture, and back into coconut mixture. Carefully drop each coated shrimp into 375 degree oil, one at a time, leaving space between each shrimp and fry until golden brown. Remove shrimp to paper towels and drain.

Sauce
Combine ½ cup piña colada drink mix, sour cream, and pineapple. Platter the shrimp and serve immediately, with sauce.

Pita Triangles

Preheat oven 350 to 400 degrees

Pita bread rounds
Butter, melted
Paprika
Garlic salt

Line a cookie sheet with foil, and place pita on top. Brush with butter and sprinkle with paprika and garlic salt. Bake for about 5 minutes, or until hot, but not burned. Watch carefully.

Remove from oven and cut into triangles, using scissors.
Serve with Fanny Farmer Sauce (see "NAUGHTY SAUCY')

Salmon Topped Potato Pancake with Caviar

Potato pancakes (see "A LITTLE SOMETHING ON THE SIDE")
Sour cream
Nova smoked salmon slices
Caviar or fresh dill

Warm pancake and top with dollop of sour cream and salmon. Top with Caviar or fresh dill and serve.

Potato pancakes are excellent if made half white potato and half sweet potato. (see "A LITTLE SOMETHING ON THE SIDE" **Combination Pancakes**)

A young girl joins an order of silence. Every five years she is brought before the Mother Superior and allowed to say two words. At the end of her first five years the Mother Superior asks "Well, my Dear, how is everything going. Remember you are only allowed to say two words"
"Cold Food" says the novice nun.
"I am so sorry" the Senior Nun said apologetically, " I will personally make sure your food is warm from now on."
Five years go by and the girl is brought to the Mother's office.
"Well my Dear" says the Mother Superior "you have been with us for ten years now. Knowing that you can only say two words is there anything you would like to say" inquires the Mother Superior.
"Hard bed" says the young nun.
"Oh my" sighs the Mother "that is terrible. We will have your mattress changed today."
Another five years go by and once again in front of the Mother Superior the young nun appears.
"Do you have anything to say in two words?" she asks
"I quit" exclaims the girl.
"Well I am not at all surprised" snorts the Mother "for fifteen years you have done nothing but bitch!!!"

Shrimp Log

Preheat oven 475 degrees
Serves 8 to 12

3 Tablespoons butter, melted
4 canned artichoke hearts, drained and halved
8 ounces fresh mushrooms, sliced
1 teaspoon parsley
1 teaspoon garlic powder
1 10x18 sheet of puff pastry
10 ounces sliced Swiss cheese
¾ pound jumbo shrimp (about 12) cooked, shelled and defined
1 egg beaten
½ teaspoon minced parsley for garnish

Melt butter in fry pan and sauté artichoke, mushrooms, parsley flakes, and garlic powder for 2 minutes. Cool and drain. Grease large cookie sheet and place puff pastry on it. Overlap cheese slices lengthwise along right half of dough. Leave an inch border along long end, and ½ inch boarder along other end. Arrange artichoke hearts on cheese spacing evenly. Layer mushrooms and cooked shrimp. Brush boarder with beaten egg. Fold left half of dough over filling, pressing edges firmly with your fingers or fork tines to seal. Reserve extra pieces of puff pastry and cut out designs. Place on top of log and brush with egg wash to adhere. (Log may be prepared up to 8 hours ahead.) Cover with foil or plastic wrap and refrigerate.

When ready to use, brush pastry with beaten egg. Bake log at 475 for 5 minutes, then reduce oven temperature to 375 and continue baking until golden, about 15 to 20 minutes. Slice and serve immediately.

Cartoon:

Man is sitting by himself in a large amphitheater.
The sign above says "Premature Ejaculation meeting"
And the guy says, "I guess I came too soon."

Spanakopetes
Greek spinach cheese triangles

Preheat oven to 425 degrees
Makes about 35

Spinach, frozen whole leaf, 10-ounce package, or fresh, 1 pound
3 Tablespoons olive oil
1 onion, finely chopped
½ pound feta cheese (from Greek grocer or gourmet shop)
6 ounces pot cheese
¼ cup parsley, chopped
1 teaspoon dried dill weed
½ teaspoon salt
⅛ teaspoon pepper
3 eggs
¼ cup corn flake crumbs
½ pound frozen Filo or Filo strudel sheets. (Keep refrigerated until ready to use.)
¼ pound butter

Defrost frozen spinach at room temperature, about 3 hours, or wash fresh spinach. Drain very thoroughly and cut up with scissors.
Squeeze between sheets of paper towel.

Heat oil in fry pan and add onions. Sauté until they become translucent. Add spinach and simmer, stirring occasionally until moisture evaporates.

Crumble corn flakes and crumble feta cheese, in a bowl. Blend in pot cheese, parsley, dill, salt & pepper.

Beat eggs and mix with cheese. Add spinach mixture and crumbs and blend thoroughly.

Defrost Filo sheets at room temperature just enough to spread sheets out. Before unrolling, cut Filo roll into thirds. Wrap ⅔ in plastic wrap and refrigerate until needed.

Wrap ⅓ in plastic wrap. Remove 1 sheet at a time to work with.

Melt butter. Lay 1 Filo sheet on a clean surface and brush liberally with butter. Fold the 2 long sides towards the middle, making a strip about 2" wide x 11" long. Brush liberally with butter again.

Place 1 tablespoon of spinach-cheese mixture in a bottom corner of strip. Fold pastry (with filling) over, so that the bottom edge meets a side edge and forms a right-angle triangle shape. Continue folding over from side to side into neat triangles until end of strip. Brush liberally with butter again.

When refrigerated pastry is needed, remove ½ at a time and wrap in dampened towel. Follow preceding process until all ingredients are used. Freeze on flat surface. Pack frozen triangles in freezer container or bag and return to freezer.

Serving Day: Place triangles on a baking pan (not a cookie sheet, because butter drips. Bake at 425 degrees for 20 to 25 minutes, turning once, until browned on both sides. Cool 5 minutes before serving.

Serve as hors d'oeuvres or as an accompaniment to soup.

Greek Cheese Pies

Preheat oven to 350 degrees
Makes 60 pies

¼ cup melted sweet butter
1 pound cottage cheese, small curd
1 beaten egg
¾ cup grated Romano cheese
1 box Filo

Keep filo frozen until ready to use. Night before using, take filo out of freezer and put in refrigerator. When using filo, keep covered in plastic wrap. Filo dough dries out quickly. Work rapidly when making the cheese pies. Do not allow edges of dough to get wet. Place filo on a clean surface and butter each sheet. Cut each sheet into strips, about 7 to 8 strips to each sheet. Mix cheeses and eggs together. Put a teaspoon of filling at each end of the filo strips. Fold as a flag. Fold first, turn in the shape of a triangle. Finish with three corners. Freeze uncooked.

Place filo triangles on a broiler pan and bake at 350 degrees or until lightly browned. Remove and drain on paper towels.

Stuffed Red Skin Potatoes

Yield 36
Preheat oven to 425 degrees

1 pound potatoes small sized #B creamers (red), washed
Melt ¼ pound of butter, cut into pieces
Assorted fillings

Place potatoes in baking pan, dot with butter, salt and pepper. As butter melts, roll potatoes around in the pan, adding more butter as needed. Bake at 425 until potato interior feels soft when you take a sharp knife and cut into the center.

When potatoes feel cool enough to handle, cut each one in half. Cut a little off the bottom of each half of potato, to allow the potato half to lay flat.

Scoop out potato insides, (reserving discarded potato for another use) being careful to leave a thin potato edge next to the skin. Season potato boats with salt, pepper, and browned butter drippings left in the bottom of the baking pan.

Fillings
Cooked crumbled bacon, cheddar cheese and mozzarella cheese, Chives and sour cream.
Caviar (prefer white fish to lump fish, if it is available) and sour cream
Chipotle southwestern dip, topped with tomatoes, scallions, taco meat, green chilies, avocado and olives, grated Mexican cheeses.
Chicken salad
Potato salad
Crab Chantilly (see below)
Cooked broccoli florets and cheddar cheese
Filet, sautéed rare and topped with Béarnaise (see "NAUGHTY SAUCY")
Taco (see "IN THE BOUEF ") meat, finely chopped onions, tomatoes, avocado, Mexican grated cheeses
Smoked salmon, cream cheese, and fresh snipped dill weed.

BUMPER STICKER
Money isn't everything, but it sure keeps the kids coming home!

Crab Chantilly Cream

Makes 1 cup

½ to ⅓ cup mayonnaise
½ cup whipped heavy cream
Dash nutmeg
Salt and pepper to taste
Dash cayenne pepper
½ to 1 pound lump crabmeat, drained (Costco or local fish market)
2 avocados
Pimento or red pepper strips, for color
Lemon juice

Cut avocados into small diced pieces, soak in lemon juice for one minute, so that the pieces won't turn brown, or simply spray with lemon juice. Add to crabmeat with the scallions, dill, salt and pepper.

Stir in just enough to coat the crab mixture.
Fill warm potato boats and serve.

Try bacon pieces or caviar, for a different taste.

The Love Dress

A gal in her sixties decides to drop in unexpectedly at her son's house. She knocks on the front door. Finding it slightly ajar, she walks in, only to find her daughter-in-law lying naked on the couch. Seeing the surprised look on her Mother-in-Law's face, she quickly explains that she is waiting for her husband to come home. When he sees her in her "love dress" he will make mad passionate love to her.

The Mother-in-Law decides to try this on her husband. She races home and drapes herself naked on the couch, when her husband arrives; he wants to know what's going on. She tells him she has on the "love dress". He says" well your love dress needs ironing! Now, when is dinner????

Surf and Turf Tenderloin Teasers

Preheat oven 400 degrees
Serves 4

¾ pound beef tenderloin, cut into 12 one ounce medallions
3 Tablespoons butter
1 Tablespoon olive oil
Salt and pepper, to taste
2 Tablespoons chopped fresh garlic (or chopped jarred garlic)
12 bite sized lobster pieces (raw or cooked Maine or slipper lobster)
Sour dough baguette, sliced thin into rounds (at least 12)
Melted butter
Garlic salt
Béarnaise sauce (see "NAUGHTY SAUCY")

Place bread rounds on a cookie sheet, and brush both sides of bread with melted butter. Sprinkle top side with garlic salt. Bake at 400 degrees, turning once, until both sides are lightly toasted. Remove from oven and wrap in aluminum foil until ready to use.

In a heavy duty fry pan, heat 3 tablespoons butter and the oil until hot, but do not allow butter to brown. Add the beef medallions, season with salt and pepper, and sear quickly for medium rare. During the last minute of cooking, add the garlic, sauté briefly, being careful not to burn. Top each bread crouton with an equal sized beef medallion.

Toss the lobster meat into the remaining garlic butter and sauté quickly either to cook raw pieces, or to warm already cooked lobster pieces. Top each beef medallion with a piece of lobster. Spoon available garlic butter evenly over medallions and top with béarnaise.

Note-- beef medallions may be served without lobster, either with béarnaise, or with the garlic butter remaining in the fry pan and topped with a pickle instead of Béarnaise.

A 2 year old little girl is really bad and for the very first time in her young life, she gets spanked, after which she retreats to her room and slams the door. When her parents don't hear from her, they start to get worried. They go upstairs and quietly open the little girl's bedroom door and peak inside. She is standing naked in front of her long mirror inspecting the area where she had been spanked. "Now you've done it!" she exclaims! "You've cracked it!!!!!!!"

Zucchini Tidbits

Makes 3 to 4 dozen small squares
Preheat oven 350 degrees

3 Zucchini, sliced
3 yellow onions, coarsely chopped
3 eggs, beaten
¼ pound Monterey Jack cheese, grated
¼ pound Mozzarella cheese, grated
¼ pound fresh grated parmesan
Olive oil

Add oil to frying pan and sauté onion and zucchini in oil until soft. Drain.

Mix eggs and cheese and stir into cooked mixture. Pour into greased 13x9 baking dish. Bake at 350 degrees for 30 minutes.

For appetizer, cut into small squares and serve.
To serve with main course, cook in large greased pie plate and serve in pie wedges.

Note-- if you are planning to freeze mixture, reduce baking time. When mixture is set, but not fully cooked, remove from oven and cool. Wrap and seal before freezing. Defrost partially, before reheating or microwaving.

An old man and his old wife are fighting constantly because their memory is awful.
They go to the doctors and he suggests they write everything down, thus taking some of
The stress out of their marriage.
That night, when they go to bed she asks him to bring her a dish of vanilla ice cream and suggests that he write it down.
He says he can remember "ice cream" but, she adds, I would like some sliced strawberries.
He is sure he can remember that much. But now she adds some nuts on top.
Still he doesn't feel the need to write anything down even though she keeps suggesting it.
Off he goes to the kitchen mumbling "ice cream, strawberries and nuts".
When he returns a few minutes later with a plate of scrambled eggs and bacon she is very frustrated and yells ...." and where is the toast?"

lettuce dress you

Asparagus Salad

Serves 6

1 bunch thin asparagus
Pinch of baking soda
Cherry or grape tomatoes, any color
Hearts of palm, sliced
Capers,
2 hard boiled eggs, chopped
1 small can sliced black olives
1 small can of artichoke hearts, not marinated (optional)

Break off the end of the first asparagus, at the tender part, line up the rest of the asparagus to the one that is cut, and slice off hard tops to make asparagus of equal length, discarding the short ends. Using an asparagus steamer or an electric fry pan with a grate, lay the asparagus tips so that they do not sit totally in water. Add a pinch of baking soda to the boiling water and steam asparagus al dente. Drain and immediately run under cold water until asparagus is cool. Drain on paper towels and refrigerate.

Just before serving, cut asparagus into thirds, arrange on platter or individual serving plates, and top colorfully with remaining ingredients, leaving the chopped egg on top. One hour ahead of serving, dress salad lightly with French dressing.

French Salad Dressing

½ cup sugar
1 teaspoon celery seed or salt
1 teaspoon paprika
2½ teaspoons grated onion
¼ cup cider vinegar
1 cup salad oil
1 clove garlic (or ½ teaspoon of jarred chopped garlic)

Shake well, but do not beat or oil will emulsify. Dressing may be made days ahead and refrigerated. Allow dressing to reach room temperature before pouring over asparagus. Salad may be dressed an hour ahead and allowed to marinate.

Balsamic Dressing

Makes 1⅔ cups

½ cup good quality Balsamic vinegar
3 Tablespoons, Dijon style mustard
1 teaspoon chopped garlic
2 small shallots, minced
¼ teaspoon salt
¼ teaspoon pepper
3 Tablespoons honey
1 cup good quality olive oil

In food processor, whisk together vinegar, mustard, garlic, salt, pepper, and honey. Gradually add oil in a steady stream.

Balsamic Vinaigrette Dressing

Makes 2 cups

¼ cup + 1 Tablespoon brown sugar
½ cup + 2 Tablespoons very good quality balsamic vinegar
¾ cup sesame oil
¾ cup + 1 Tablespoon olive oil
1 teaspoon chopped garlic
1½ Tablespoons granulated chicken bouillon (not cube form)

Mix above ingredients together, refrigerate and save. When ready to serve, microwave for 40 seconds until fat is dissolved. Use electric hand emulsifier blender or shake vigorously.

**A man is having an affair with his secretary. He wakes up after they have spent the day together and realizes how late it has gotten. He racks his brain for an excuse to tell his wife. Finally he says to his girlfriend "Hurry, take my sneakers and rub them in the grass until they are really stained, while I get dressed."
When he gets home, he is greeted by his wife with "AND WHERE WERE YOU???" "Having an affair with my secretary" replies the unfaithful husband.
"Yeah right" says the irate wife eyeing his sneakers, "you've been out playing golf, again!"**

Bruschetta Seashell Pasta Salad

Serves 6 to 8

- 1 ¼ lb. or more fresh ripe tomatoes, chopped (heirloom, organic vine-ripe, or plums work best)
- 4 cloves fresh garlic (or 2 teaspoons jarred)
- 30 large fresh basil leaves, chopped, no stems
- ½ cup olive oil
- 1 teaspoon salt
- 1 teaspoon pepper
- 1 lb. medium seashell pasta, cooked and drained
- ½ lb. or more whole milk grated or shredded mozzarella cheese
- 6 ounces pitted black olives (optional)
- Pepperoni and other personal favorites (optional)
- 1 Tablespoon salad oil

24 hours ahead, marinate tomatoes in olive oil, basil, salt & pepper.
3 hours before serving, add garlic to tomato marinade.

Boil water, add salt and salad oil. Add 1 pound medium seashell pasta and cook according to package directions, stirring pasta half way through cooking time. Drain but do not rinse.

While pasta is hot, stir in grated mozzarella. Cheese will get stringy as it melts, but do not allow cheese to clump together. When cheese is melted, add tomato mixture.

Note-- when mixing salad together, sometimes the cheese gets too stringy. Have cheese at room temperature and the pasta shells not too hot.

**A man goes to take a shower after his round of golf only to find that the men's shower is broken. The Pro shop suggests that he use the Ladies Room, as all the women are gone home. As he is drying off, he hears three women enter the Ladies Room. Not knowing whether to wrap the towel around his head or his waist, he covers his head and makes a dash for the door. One woman turns to the others and says "well, that wasn't my husband"!
The second woman says "It wasn't my husband either"!
The third woman says "He isn't even a Member of the Club!!"**

Chicken Endive & Roquefort Salad

Serves 10 to 12

10 boneless chicken breasts, grilled (or rotisserie roasted, white meat only, boneless, cubed)
1 large bunch romaine lettuce (or substitute curly endive)
4 Belgian endive heads cut into 1 inch pieces
8 ounces Roquefort cheese, crumbled
1½ bunches radishes, thinly sliced
1½ cups walnuts, chopped
Bermuda or Vidalia onion, sliced thin
Mustard vinaigrette dressing

Mustard Vinaigrette Dressing
4 teaspoons Dijon mustard
2 ounce can of anchovies, drained & minced
¼ cup red wine vinegar
⅔ cup olive oil
2 green onions, minced, include green tops
1½ teaspoon dried thyme, crumbled
Freshly ground pepper

In food processor bowl, combine mustard, anchovies, onions, thyme, and pepper. Whisk in vinegar. With processor on high, start adding oil slowly, in steady stream, and continue to process until oil is emulsified. Add onions, thyme, and pepper and continue to process. Dressing may be prepared 3 days ahead of time and refrigerated. Allow dressing to reach room temperature or microwave briefly and shake well before serving.

Break washed lettuce into bite sized pieces and place in large salad bowl or individual cold salad plates and top with sliced radishes, crumbled Roquefort, nuts, and onion. This may be prepared 3 hours ahead of time, covered with plastic wrap and refrigerated.

Just before serving, add grilled or Rotisserie chicken cubes, walnuts, and dressing. Toss to coat.

Chicken Spiral Pasta Salad

Serves 10 to 12

1 box spiral pasta
Roasted chicken, boneless and skinless, white meat only, cubed (tuna, ham, prosciutto or pepperoni, may be substituted)
4 hard boiled eggs, sliced
½ small onion, chopped
1 cup celery, chopped (3 to 4 stalks)
4 to 6 ounces of parmesan cheese, grated
Small amount of olive oil
Salt

Chicken Pasta Salad Dressing
2 cups mayonnaise
2 cups sour cream
½ teaspoon salt
½ teaspoon pepper
2 Tablespoons, plus 1 teaspoon oregano, or to taste
1 additional cup sour cream
1 additional cup mayonnaise

At least 24 hours before serving, combine ingredients for salad, except for the additional sour cream and mayonnaise, which should be added just before serving.

Fill a large pasta pot with water. Add olive oil, salt and bring to rapid boil. Add pasta and cook 14 minutes, or until desired tenderness. Drain and rinse in cold water.

Place cooled pasta in a large salad bowl. Add all ingredients (except for sour cream and mayonnaise to be added just before serving) and toss with dressing. The day of serving, adjust all seasonings, adding more mayonnaise and sour cream as needed.

To use poached chicken, instead of rotisserie chicken (see "A FARE TO REMEMBER" **HOT CHICKS, Poached Chicken**)

Cobb Salad with Blue Cheese Dressing

Serves 3

Cobb Salad
Spring mix greens or red and green leafy lettuce
1 can of corn, drained (or fresh corn on the cob steamed and cut off the cob)
2 plum tomatoes
Avocado, sliced or cubed
4 slices cooked bacon
3 ounces of crumbled blue cheese or gorgonzola cheese
8 ounces of grilled or roasted chicken or cooked shrimp

Blue Cheese Dressing
4 ounces blue cheese or gorgonzola cheese
1 cup sour cream
1 teaspoon Worcestershire sauce
1 teaspoon fresh lemon juice
¼ cup Wishbone Italian dressing
Garlic & salt to taste

Mix well with fork. Chill.

Note-- if using crumbled blue cheese or gorgonzola cheese on the salad, only use 3 ounces of cheese in dressing and 1 ounce or more crumbled on the salad.

Main Entrée- for dinner, use about ⅓ to ½ pound of shrimp or chicken per person.

A golfer hits his ball into the beautiful field of buttercups.
He is about to hit the ball out, when stops his swing, takes an unplayable lie, and carefully removes the ball from the buttercups. With that, lightening strikes and Mother Nature's voice appears!
"You are the only golfer to ever care about the beauty of my buttercups and for that, my son, you will have free butter for the rest of your life, and the butter will be plentiful.
"Where were you when my golf ball went into the "Pussy willows" screams the golfer?

Deviled Egg Salad

Serves 4

7 eggs, boiled (see "Helps")
1 Tablespoon plus 2 teaspoons very finely chopped sweet onion.
¼ teaspoon curry
¼ teaspoon Grey Poupon mustard
Speck of horseradish
½ cup mayonnaise
Dash of pickle relish
Salt and pepper, to taste

Peel eggs and allow to cool. Place yolks and chopped onion in food processor or mini chopper and pulse till fluffy. Chop whites by hand. Add all ingredients together and toss lightly.

Deviled Eggs as Appetizer
Place yolk mixture in a baggie. Cut off the tip of the bottom corner of the baggie. Flute the egg yolk mixture into the center of the egg white. Top with sprinkled paprika or fresh parsley sprig.

A guy finds himself playing golf with a man who sights his golf ball through the sights of a gun. He has never seen this before and asks the man what he does for a living.
"I am a paid assassin" he replies.
"What do you charge?" asks the man and the assassin replies: "$1,000 per person".
"I suspect my wife is having an affair with my neighbor. Actually I live on this golf hole. You can see my house through your gun scope".
He borrows the gun and looks into the bedroom of his house where he sees his wife and his neighbor.
The man agrees to the assassin's $2,000 fee. $1,000 for his wife and $1,000 for his neighbor.
The assassin sights the gun and keeps going back and forth between the two targets.
"What are you waiting for?" asks the impatient husband.
The assassin says "Give me a second, I think I can save you $1,000 !!!

Exotic Chicken Salad

Serves 4

1 large Rotisserie roasted chicken, white meat, boneless, cubed
1½ ounce package, sliced almonds
1 cup mayonnaise
½ Tablespoon curry powder
1 Tablespoon soy sauce
1 Tablespoon lemon juice
2 stalks celery, chopped
1½ – 6 ounce cans water chestnuts, chopped
½ to 1 pounds seedless green grapes, quartered
Boston or Bibb lettuce

Coat almond slivers with melted butter and spread on foiled cookie sheet. Bake at 300 for 30 minutes, or until lightly brown.

Several hours before serving, mix mayonnaise with curry powder, soy sauce and lemon juice. Combine chicken, celery, water chestnuts and grapes, and add only enough curried mayonnaise as needed for the salad. Salad may be prepared at least 24 hours ahead. Chill. Mound onto lettuce leaves, sprinkle with toasted almonds and serve.

Note-- Pineapple chunks, fresh pitted cherries, or champagne red grapes may be used instead of seedless green grapes, but grapes are the best.

Tarragon Chicken Salad

Serves 4

1 large Rotisserie roasted chicken, white meat, boneless, cubed
2 stalks celery, chopped
½ cup sour cream
½ cup mayonnaise
1 Tablespoon tarragon
Salt and pepper, to taste
½ cup walnuts, chopped

Combine sour cream, mayonnaise, tarragon, salt, pepper, and tarragon. Mix chicken cubes, celery and nuts. Add only enough mayonnaise as needed. If salad gets dry, add more mayonnaise mixture, Stir and refrigerate until ready to use.

Flaming Hot Spinach Salad

Serves 4 to 6

1 package fresh baby spinach, washed
6 thick strips of rendered bacon (save bacon fat)
½ cup bacon fat
1 clove fresh garlic, chopped
Salt & pepper, to taste
1 ripe peach skinned and cubed (see "Help")
1 ripe nectarine skinned and cubed (see Help")
4 ounces sliced and washed mushrooms
1 ripe avocado, peeled and cubed
1 pound shrimp (size 21 to 25 to the pound), raw, peeled, and deveined (may substitute cold, boiled, peeled and deveined)
Cherry tomatoes, chopped
Toasted pine nuts
Butter

Vinaigrette Dressing
2 Tablespoons sugar
2 Tablespoons light brown sugar, packed
2 Tablespoons Worcestershire sauce
4 Tablespoons vinegar raspberry vinegar (suggest 4 Monks brand, pomegranate vinegar or cider vinegar, may be substituted)
1½ ounces Cognac Brandy
1 teaspoon green pepper Tabasco sauce

Wash & break leaves of spinach into bite-sized pieces. Add salt and pepper to taste, plus lemon juice.

Preheat oven to 300 degrees. Line cookie sheet with foil and place pine nuts on top. Top with pats of butter and bake nuts 300 degrees. Watch nuts carefully, as they will burn easily.

Cook bacon crisp, place bacon on a paper towel to drain. Add butterflied shrimp and fry in hot bacon grease. Remove shrimp discard all but ½ cup bacon fat. Add chopped garlic and sauté. Remove garlic and add vinaigrette dressing to remaining bacon fat and heat over medium flame. Reduce slightly and pour hot dressing over leaves. Add brandy to fry pan and warm over medium heat. Avert eyes and ignite with long handled match. Pour flaming brandy over leaves. Top with peaches, nectarines, avocado, mushrooms, tomatoes, shrimp, avocado, and toasted pine nuts. Toss, adjust seasonings, and serve immediately.

French Silk Potato Salad to Die For

Serves 5

½ cup mayonnaise
¼ cup sour cream
1 teaspoon salt
1 Tablespoon cider vinegar
2 Tablespoons olive oil
2 teaspoons Grey Poupon mustard
1 Tablespoon sugar
¼ cup chopped parsley

(The above ingredients can be mixed days ahead and refrigerated for several days)

6 strips bacon
¾ cups chopped scallions, including green tops
2 pounds red skin creamers "size B" potatoes, washed, leaving skin on

Sauté 6 strips of bacon. Remove from pan and drain, saving the bacon fat to cook the scallions. Sauté ¾ cups of chopped scallions in remaining bacon fat just before you are ready to use.

Add potatoes to boiling salted water to cover. Cook covered on high for approximately 40 minutes, remove and drain when tender.

While hot, cut potatoes into quarters and place in a bowl. Add crumbled bacon, and all hot bacon fat with sautéed scallions. Add the mayonnaise mixture and toss.

Serve immediately.

After refrigerating, salad can be covered and reheated in microwave on low reheat heat, just take the "chill" off the salad. Salad tastes best served at room temperature.

What's the difference between a northern zoo and a southern zoo?
A northern zoo has a plaque on each cage describing the animal in it.
A southern zoo has a plaque on the front of each cage describing the animal in it and the recipe for it.

Fresh Broccoli Mandarin Salad

Serves 10 to12

Salad Ingredients
4 cups fresh broccoli florets, cut into small bite size pieces and steamed
½ cup raisins
6 slices bacon, cooked and crumbled
2 cups sliced fresh mushrooms
½ cup slivered almonds, toasted
1 cans (11 ounce) mandarin oranges, drained
½ cup large red onion, sliced

Place broccoli stems in bottom of steamer pot strainer. Top with broccoli florets and place over small amount of boiling, salted water. Add a pinch of baking powder to the water, and steam covered, until florets are tender, about 6 minutes.

Sweet and Sour Hollandaise Dressing
1 egg, plus one egg yolk, lightly beaten
½ cup granulated sugar
1½ teaspoons corn starch
1 teaspoon dry mustard
¼ cup tarragon vinegar
¼ cup water
3 Tablespoons butter, softened
½ cup mayonnaise

In top of double boiler, whisk together egg, egg yolk, sugar, cornstarch and mustard. Combine vinegar and water. Slowly pour into egg mixture, whisking constantly. Place over hot water and cook, stirring constantly until thick. Remove from heat. Add butter. Pour into food processor (dough blade) and add mayonnaise. Blend and pour into container. Cool, cover and refrigerate.

Dressing can be made well ahead of time and stored in refrigerator.

Just before serving, toss salad ingredients with dressing.

Note-- to serve as Entrée, add cooked chicken (see **Poached Chicken** "WILD CHICKS") or rotisserie chicken, boneless white meat only, or boiled or woked shrimp. Marinate in dressing before adding to salad.

Granny Smith Salad with Balsamic Dressing

Serves 3

1 package of spring mix (baby greens)
1 Granny Smith unpeeled, cored. Thinly sliced, and sprayed lightly with lemon juice.
3 ounces crumbled gorgonzola cheese
Chicken, shrimp, or salmon – optional
Walnuts, chopped (toasting is optional)
Balsamic dressing (see" **Balsamic Dressing** "LETTUCE DRESS YOU")

Combine all the above ingredients, and dress lightly with balsamic vinaigrette salad dressing.

Note-- When in season, instead of Granny Smith apples, this salad is delicious with thinly sliced nectarines, peaches, whole raspberries, crumbled gorgonzola cheese; Meringue baked pecans (see "HOT NUTS") and tossed with balsamic salad dressing.

Baby Blue Salad

Serves 3

1 package of spring mix salad greens
3 ounces blue cheese, crumbled
1 orange, peeled and cut into thin slices
1 pint strawberries, sliced
Sweet-and-spicy pecans (see "HOT NUTS")
Balsamic dressing (see **Balsamic Dressing** "LETTUCE DRESS YOU")

Sign on Church Marquis
The sermon this morning: "Jesus walks on water"
The sermon tonight "Searching for Jesus"

Greek Orzo Salad

Preheat oven to 300 degrees
Serves 6

1 cup orzo uncooked pasta
6 cherry tomatoes cut in quarters
¼ cup sweet onions, chopped
¼ cup celery or water chestnuts, diced
1 bunch fresh basil leaves, chopped (no stems)
2 Tablespoons finely chopped, pitted Kalamata olives
1½ Tablespoon capers
1 teaspoon grainy Dijon mustard
1 Tablespoon good quality balsamic vinegar
¼ teaspoon sugar
2 teaspoons garlic oil (if this is not available, marinate whole pieces of garlic in olive oil for several hours, discarding the garlic but saving 2 teaspoons of garlic flavored oil.
Salt
Pepper, fresh ground
3½ ounces Chevre (goat cheese), crumbled
Toasted pine nuts

Foil cookie sheet and top with pine nuts and pats of butter. Bake nuts at 300 degrees, until lightly browned. Watch carefully, as they will burn quickly.

Cook orzo, following package directions until al dente. Drain and cool. Toss pasta with tomatoes, onions, basil, celery or water chestnuts, capers, and olives

Vinaigrette
Whisk together the mustard, sugar, and vinegar. In a steady stream, beat in oil. Pour this vinaigrette over the pasta mixture and season to taste. Refrigerate.

Before serving, top with crumbled Chevre and pine nuts.

If Monica Lewinsky married the UNABOMBER, Ted Kaczynski, her name would be:
Monica Lewinsky Kaczynski and it would be a hell of a blow job!

Greek Pasta Salad

Serves 10

Salad Ingredients
1 large head romaine lettuce
1 head Iceberg lettuce
Greek black olives
Grape tomatoes, halved
Halved artichoke hearts
Red pepper strips, julienne
Greek peppers
Hearts of palm, sliced
Crumbled goat cheese
1 pound cooked, rinsed, and cooled angel hair pasta
Roasted or grilled chicken, shrimp or scallops (optional)

Fill pasta pot with lots of water. Over high heat, bring water to a rapid boil. Add salt and olive oil to keep pasta from sticking together. Break pasta into thirds, and drop into boiling water. Cook as to package directions, stirring half way through suggested cooking time or until tender. Remove from heat, drain and rinse.

Greek Vinaigrette Yields approximately 1¾ cups dressing
¼ cup Grey Poupon Dijon Mustard
½ Tablespoon dry mustard
1 Tablespoon oregano
1 Tablespoon granulated garlic or ½ tablespoon chopped garlic
½ Tablespoon paprika
3/8 teaspoon cracked black pepper
3/8 teaspoon salt
2 ¾ Tablespoons sugar
1¼ Tablespoons lemon juice
1¼ Tablespoons soy sauce
1 cup vegetable oil
½ cup red wine vinegar

Put all ingredients (except oil) in food processor. While processing, add oil a little at a time and then in a steady stream.

Sour Cream Dressing Yields approximately 3 cups
1 egg
2 cups salad oil
½ cup red wine vinegar

continued

½ Tablespoon Worcestershire sauce
½ teaspoon chopped fresh garlic
Pepper, a pinch or two
½ Tablespoon grated Asiago cheese (or fresh parmesan)
½ teaspoon salt
1 Tablespoon sour cream
Louisiana pepper sauce, one shake or to taste

Put eggs and vinegar in a food processor; blend until mixture doubles in volume, approximately 1 minute. With the processor running, add oil in a thin, steady stream until mixture thickens.

Scrape into bowl and, in the order listed above, blend in the balance of the ingredients. Adjust seasonings to taste. Pour into storage container and refrigerate.

Greek Pasta Dressing
Combine about 2 ½ cups of Sour Cream Dressing with 1 to 1 ½ cups of Greek Vinaigrette Dressing depending on your desired taste. Consistency should be thick and creamy.

Toss cooked pasta with 1 cup of combined dressings, reserving the remaining dressing. Refrigerate the remaining dressing and the dressed pasta for at least 3 hours.

Assemble Salad
Break washed and dried lettuce, into bite sized pieces and arrange on serving platter or individual cold salad plates. Top with marinated pasta and remaining salad ingredients. Lightly drizzle salad with Greek Pasta Dressing and serve additional dressing on the side. For an interesting presentation, buy extra long pasta and cook as above until tender. Drain and rinse. Using pasta as a hank (like yarn) makes a knot in the center and top salad. Add cooked meat or seafood.

A husband and wife were celebrating their 25th Wedding Anniversary.
At her request they returned to the same Hotel they had spent their Honeymoon in.
She puts her arms around him and said "25 years ago you were a Greek God to me, now you are just a God damned Greek".

Heirloom Tomato Salad

Preheat oven 300 degrees

Heirloom tomatoes, thickly sliced
Fresh mozzarella, thickly sliced
Fresh basil leaves, cut in small pieces
Gorgonzola cheese, crumbled
Salt
Toasted pine nuts
Butter
Balsamic dressing (see Balsamic Dressing "LETTUCE US DRESS YOU")

Foil cookie sheet and spread pine nut evenly. Top with pats of butter and bake in 300 degree oven till lightly browned. Remove and set aside.

On a large platter or individual serving plates, overlap tomatoes slices with mozzarella slices and season with salt, to taste. Top with basil, cheese, and nuts. Dribble with balsamic dressing, or just good quality olive oil and balsamic vinegar, and serve.

Colorful Tomatoes

Red and yellow heirloom tomatoes cut into wedges
Sweet onion, cut very thin
Fresh marinated mozzarella balls (Costco is best source)
1 can artichokes, not marinated, drained and cut into wedges
Small black olives, pitted
Salt, to taste
Feta cheese, crumbled, optional
Crisp, cooked bacon, optional
Favorite Italian dressing

Place ingredients in a large serving bowl. Add dressing and salt. Cover and refrigerate until ready to serve.

Shrimp and Avocado Salad

Serves 5 to 6

1 pound shrimp, cooked, peeled, and deveined (21 to 25 per pound)
Lemon juice
1 cup sour cream
3 Tablespoons ketchup
1 cup plus 3 Tablespoons mayonnaise
3 Tablespoons orange juice
1 Tablespoon Cognac, or to taste
Cayenne pepper, dash
Salt and pepper, to taste
Avocado, diced
Pistachios, shelled and chopped
Mandarin orange slices or melon balls (cantaloupe and honeydew)
Fresh sprigs of dill, for decoration
Bibb or Boston lettuce leaves

Spray cold, cooked shrimp with a little lemon juice.

Mix together, sour cream, mayonnaise, ketchup, orange juice, Cognac, cayenne pepper, salt, and pepper. Place shrimp and diced avocado in a bowl. Add enough sauce to marinate. Cover and refrigerate for 1 hour.

Spread lettuce leaves on serving platter or individual plates. Top with shrimp, avocado, and pistachios. Distribute the orange slices or melon balls and decorate with sprigs of dill. Dribble with sauce and serve. Mixture may also be served out of a lettuce lined bowl.

**Two women are playing golf, when they see a streaker run across the fairway.
"Is that Dick Green" asks on of the two?
"No, just a reflection off the grass" replies the other one.**

Shrimp and Mandarin Salad

Serves 12

2½ pounds shrimp (21 to 25 to the pound) cooked, cleaned and Deveined
6 oranges, peeled and sliced (may substitute Mandarin oranges)
5 medium sweet onions, sliced very thin
Bibb or Boston lettuce

Mandarin Salad Dressing
1½ cup cider vinegar
1 cup lemon juice
1 cup vegetable oil
½ cup ketchup
¼ cup sugar
2 teaspoons dried pepper flakes
2 teaspoons parsley, finely chopped
1½ teaspoons, salt
2 teaspoons mustard seed
1 teaspoon celery seed
½ teaspoon, pepper
2 cloves garlic, crushed

Mix dressing and add shrimp, onions, and oranges. Cover and refrigerate, marinating ingredients for several hours or overnight. When ready to serve, drain, and reserve marinade.

Arrange lettuce on cold individual salad plates, or place in a large salad bowl. Top with shrimp, oranges slices, and onions. Drizzle with dressing and serve.

***Note*--** salad may also be made with raw, peeled and deveined shrimp. Just before serving, add a little sesame oil to a fry pan or wok, and stir fry shrimp. Add warm shrimp to salad ingredients, and toss with salad dressing. For a spicier dish, wok shrimp in ½ sesame oil and ½ Mongolian Fire oil (ethnic isle in grocery store).

Spicy Peanut Pasta Salad

Serves 5

¼ cup vegetable oil
3 Tablespoons sesame oil
½ teaspoon crushed red pepper
3 Tablespoons honey
1 Tablespoon soy sauce
1 teaspoon salt
8 ounces linguini
Red and green leafy lettuce
Avocados
Pear tomatoes, halved
Crushed peanuts
Olive oil

Fill a large pasta pot with water, salt and a little olive oil. Bring to a rapid boil. Break linguini noodles into thirds and place in boiling water and stir, making sure pasta does not stick together. Cook for 13 minutes, uncovered, stirring at 6 minutes. Drain and rinse with cold water

In a small sauce pan, add sesame oil, vegetable oil, and red pepper flakes. Cook for 2 to 4 minutes over medium heat. Flakes will start to float to the top. Do not allow flakes to burn. Remove from heat.

In a large bowl, mix together soy sauce, honey and salt. Add hot oil to mixture. Beat together. Stir in *cooled*, cooked linguini and marinate at least 24 hours in the refrigerator.

Tear leafy lettuce into bite sized pieces and arrange on serving platter. Drain marinated noodles and arrange on top of lettuce. Spray peeled avocado slices with lemon juice to keep from turning brown, and ring around pasta with tomatoes. Dribble with **Ginger Vinaigrette Dressing** (see below) but do not toss. Top with crushed peanuts.

Bill Clinton has created the 11th Commandment:

Thou shall not comfort thy Rod with thy Staff.

Ginger Vinaigrette Dressing

2 Tablespoons lemon juice
1½ Tablespoons soy sauce
1½ Tablespoons white vinegar
¾ teaspoon minced garlic
3½ teaspoons sugar
2½ Tablespoons olive oil
2½ Tablespoons sesame oil
⅞ teaspoon ground ginger

Food process the above ingredients, adding oil last in a steady stream.

Arrange drained linguini over leafy greens. Top with sliced avocado, tomatoes, and crushed peanuts. Top lightly with dressing, but do not toss.

Mr. Brown has been by his wife's hospital bed for weeks, but she has failed to come out of a coma.
The mystified Doctors meet with him.
"We have a suggestion" says the head Doctor.
"We have noticed that your wife's vital signs go way up when the nurses are giving her a sponge bath".
"We think if you would have oral sex with your wife, you might be able to bring her out of her coma"
"OH" says the husband "I'd be too embarrassed, to do that"
The doctors explain that the curtains will be closed around the bed. There will be complete privacy. The doctors will just be watching the monitors.
So the husband reluctantly agrees.
After about 5 minutes behind the curtains, the bells and whistles go off and her heart line is flat
Mr. Brown comes running out and so do the doctors.
"What happened" asked the doctors?
"I think she choked" said Mr. Brown.

Spinach Daisy Salad

Serves 6 to 8

2 pounds of fresh baby spinach
4 boiled eggs, sliced in rings, like daisies
1 box fresh bean sprouts
8 slices cooked and crumbled bacon
1 can water chestnuts, sliced
1 pound sliced fresh mushrooms

Spinach Salad Dressing
4 egg yolks
1 teaspoon dry mustard
1 teaspoon salt
¼ teaspoon fresh white (or black) pepper
½ cup oil
1 Tablespoons sugar
3 Tablespoons red wine vinegar
3 Tablespoons lemon juice (½ lemon)

Beat eggs yolks in a food processor, blender, or electric mixer, until light and lemon colored. Add mustard, salt, and pepper and blend well.

Add oil, a drop at a time; then continue adding oil, slowly, in a steady stream, beating until thick. Add sugar, vinegar, and lemon juice. Mix well. Dressing may be made ahead of time and refrigerated.

Arrange salad on individual cold salad plates or place in a large salad bowl. Toss with dressing and decorate with sliced eggs to look like daisies.

There is a big controversy on the Jewish view of when life begins. In Jewish tradition, the fetus is not considered viable until it graduates from medical school.

Strawberry Banana Jell-O Mold

1 large package strawberry banana Jell-O
1 large can crushed pineapple, drained
1½ cups boiling water
3 to 4 bananas, mashed in food processor or by hand with a fork
8 ounces sour cream
Small container sliced frozen strawberries, unthawed
Chopped walnuts or pecans
Greased mold

Make Jell-O according to package directions. Stir in drained pineapple, mashed bananas, chopped nuts, adding strawberries last.

Pour ½ mixtures into greased Jell-O mold. When Jell-O is set, spread the sour cream on top. Sour cream layer should be about 3/8 to ¼ thick. Top with the rest of the Jell-O mixture, spooning it on carefully. Cover and refrigerate. Unmold when ready to serve.

Raspberry Jell-O Mold

Greased ring mold
1 small raspberry Jell-O or black raspberry Jell-O
1 small lemon Jell-O
1 box frozen raspberries
1 can mandarin oranges drain and reserve juice
8 ounces cream cheese, cubed

Mix 1 cup boiling water and *raspberry Jell-O*. When dissolved, add frozen raspberries. Break up to defrost. Pour immediately into greased mold. Refrigerate to set. When Jell-O is firm, top with the small cream cheese cubes and drained mandarin oranges sections.

In a separate bowl, place package of *lemon Jell-O*, and add 1 cup boiling water. When dissolved, add ¾ cup of reserved mandarin orange juice liquid. If there is not enough mandarin orange juice to equal ¾ cup, fill with water. Cover and refrigerate until thick and partially set. Spoon Jell-O over cream cheese and orange sections, cover and refrigerate 24 hours, or until firm. Unmold and serve. Decorate platter with orange sections and fresh raspberries.

Strawberry – Spinach Salad

Serves 8

1 package baby spinach leaves and ½ iceberg lettuce
2 cups sliced strawberries
1 can sliced water chestnuts, drained
1 can Mandarin oranges, drained
Meringue Baked Pecans (see "HOT NUTS")

Combine all ingredients in a large salad bowl or arrange on individual cold salad plates and toss lightly with strawberry spinach salad dressing.

Strawberry Spinach Salad Dressing

Combine the following in a food processor:
¼ cup sugar
1 Tablespoon poppy seeds
1½ teaspoon onion, grated
½ teaspoon Worcestershire sauce
¼ teaspoon paprika
½ cup salad oil
¼ cup cider vinegar

Slowly add ½ cup salad oil and ¼ cup cider vinegar to running food processor

Also good with nectarines and/or peaches, sliced thin with skins on, If you wish to peel the fruit, blanch quickly in boiling water, place in plastic baggie and seal. Skins will come off easily. If you are not going to use the slices immediately, spray or dip into lemon juice to keep from turning brown.

All the children were in line for lunch at the Catholic elementary school. At the beginning of the food line, there was a large pile of apples. A nun had posted a note on the apple tray that said "Take ONE apple only! GOD is WATCHING!!!
At the end of the buffet line there was a pile of cookies and a child had posted a note saying "Take all the cookies you want, God is watching the apples!!!"

Raspberry Pear Spinach Salad

Preheat oven 350 degrees
Serves 8

2 packages baby spinach leaves
2 red pears sliced, skin on
2 yellow Asian pears, peeled and sliced
8 ounces crumbled gorgonzola cheese
Toasted pecans (see "HOT NUTS")

Raspberry Salad Dressing

Use Strawberry spinach salad dressing, substituting Four Monks Raspberry vinegar for cider vinegar.

Note-- for a change of pace, add strawberries, raspberries, blackberries, nectarines, peaches, any pear variety, and your choice of nuts

The police are called for a domestic disturbance.
They find a man dead on the floor, with a bloody 5 iron next to him.
"Are you his wife" the policeman asks the woman standing over the body.
"Yes" she says.
"Is this your 5 iron" the policeman asks?
"Yes" says the wife.
"Did you hit your husband" asks the policeman?
"Yes" she replied.
"How many times did you hit him" asks the policeman?
"Oh it was 4 or 5 times. No, maybe it was six. Oh what the hell put me down for a 5"!!!!

Summer Salad

Serves 10

1 head fresh broccoli florets, raw, bite sized pieces
1 head cauliflower, raw, bite sized pieces
1 medium sized zucchini, peeled, cut in 4 long strips, and slice
2 red delicious apples, with peel left on
1 quart strawberries, sliced in half
½ cup raisins, white or golden
¾ cup walnuts (or pecans), chopped
2 bananas, sliced just before serving

All the above ingredients, except for the apples, bananas, and the nuts, may be mixed together as far ahead as 24 hours, covered, marinated in the summer salad dressing and refrigerated until ready to serve. When ready to serve, place all the ingredients in a large salad bowl. Leaving the peel on, cut the apples into bite sized pieces, add to salad along with the bananas, and nuts. Toss and serve. Add more dressing if necessary.

Summer Salad Dressing

⅓ cup red wine vinegar
¾ cup sugar
1 teaspoon salt
1 teaspoon dry mustard
1 small scallion, chopped including greens
2 Tablespoon poppy seeds
1 cup vegetable oil

Place all ingredients in a jar and either shake well or blend with a hand emulsifying blender, when ready to serve. Toss above salad with dressing and serve.

A couple has three beautiful daughters. When their third baby arrives, the husband is horrified. "We have two gorgeous children, how could we have such an ugly child? Have you been fooling around"? "Not this time," the wife replies.

Tahoe Salad

Preheat oven to 300 degrees
Serves 3

¾ pound large raw shrimp, peeled, and deveined (15 to 25 / pound)
1 bag spring mix salad greens
⅓ each, roasted red, yellow, and orange peppers (skinless)
Grape tomatoes, yellow and red
3 ounces goat cheese
Toasted pine nuts (see "HOT NUTS")
½ Tablespoon sesame oil
½ Tablespoon Mongolian fire oil (ethnic aisle of grocery store)
1 Tablespoon butter, for the shrimp
Pats of butter, for the nuts
Wok, preferably with a collar
Balsamic dressing (see **Balsamic Dressing** "LETTUCE DRESS YOU")

Line a cookie sheet with foil and spread nuts evenly on pan. Top with pats of butter and bake slowly at 300 degrees, for about 10 minutes or until lightly browned. Watch nuts carefully, as they will burn easily.

Turn burner or grill on high and roast peppers directly on the burner, until the skins turn black, continually rotating the peppers. Place blackened peppers in a plastic bag and seal the baggie. The peppers will continue to steam. Remove peppers and rub the blackened skin off, using a sharp knife where necessary.

Place wok on collar over high heat and add both oils. Drop shrimp into the hot oils and stir fry until shrimp turn pink in color and are white inside. Put butter on top of shrimp and stir until melted.

Place greens on individual cold plates, or in a large salad serving bowl. Decorate with julienne peppers, colored pear tomatoes, and shrimp. Top hot shrimp with goat cheese, so that the cheese melts onto the shrimp. Sprinkle salad with toasted pine nuts and toss with balsamic salad dressing, or dressing of choice, and serve.

Wild Rice & Crab Salad

Serves 5

4 ounces (½ package) white and wild rice
12 ounces back fin lump crab meat, drained
6 ounces shrimp, cooked and peeled, and deveined
½ cup tiny peas, cooked
½ cup sweet onions, chopped
½ cup mayonnaise
1 Tablespoon lemon juice
1 teaspoon curry powder

Follow package directions to cook rice, being careful not to lift the pot lid until cooking time has been completed. Cool.

Cut shrimp into bite sized pieces. Combine crab, shrimp, peas and onions. Stir lightly. Add rice.

Combine mayonnaise, lemon juice and curry. Stir into mixture.

Cover and refrigerate. Best when made at least several hours ahead of serving

Three men show up Saturday morning for their regular golf game. Their fourth canceled and they find themselves playing with a girl. However, she turns out not only to be really beautiful but to be a terrific golfer.
They were about to putt on the 18th green when she realizes that if she makes the putt, she will break par, which she has never done before.
She turns to the golfers and says:
"I will sleep with which ever one of you that can best help me read this tricky putt and sink it"
The 1st guy says "It's going to break a little to the right at the hole."
The 2nd guy says "No, it's going to break slightly left of the hole"
The third guy says "I think it's a gimme"!!!!!!!!

nooners

California Roll Ups

Spread
16 ounces cream cheese, softened
1 package Good Seasons Italian salad mix
1 four ounce jar pimento, drained and chopped
½ cup real mayonnaise

Mix above ingredients until smooth. Cover and chill for several hours or overnight.

Roll Ups
1 package soft flour burrito

Lay out burritos individually, and spread evenly with cream cheese mixture. Cover with desired filling and roll up tightly, wrap in plastic wrap and refrigerate while you are working on the rest of the burritos, or until ready to slice and serve.

Suggested assorted fillings
Havarti cheese slices, sweet onion finely chopped, and chopped plum tomatoes.
Thin ham slices and medium sharp cheddar, shredded and alfalfa sprouts.
Crisp crumbled bacon, alfalfa sprouts, and chopped plum tomatoes.
Crab salad, diced avocado, crisp crumbled bacon and alfalfa sprouts.

Note-- you may substitute Rondele or Boursin cheese spread instead of cream cheese mixture. Any combination of meats and cheeses will work, as long as they will roll easily. Hollowed out French bread, leaving ½ inch thick bread walls, may be stuffed with spread, wrapped, chilled, and sliced when ready to serve.

When ready to serve, unroll and using an electric knife, thickly slice rolls on the diagonal and place slices on a serving platter. Sometimes the ends of the roll ups won't stick together. If this happens, use a little of the cream cheese mixture, as glue, to keep the rolls together.

One day, a man come home for lunch and is greeted by his wife dressed in a very SEXY nightie.
"Tie me up," she says seductively "and you can do anything you want."
So he tied her up and went golfing.

Crock Pot Cheese Soup

2 pounds cheddar cheese, cubed
2 cans cream of celery soup
1 can Guinness Stout
1 can regular beer

Place all ingredients in a crock pot on high until cheese has melted. Stir soup until creamy and serve.

Leek and Potato Soup

Makes about 6 cups

6 leeks
4 Tablespoons butter
3 Tablespoons fresh parsley, chopped
2 boxes beef or chicken broth or demi glaze (better taste and less salty)
1 can cream, milk, half and half, or water
3 to 4 potatoes, sliced
Celery salt and pepper, to taste
2 hard boiled eggs, chopped
3 strips thick bacon, cooked crisp and chopped

Slice leeks thin (include some of the green tops). Melt butter in large fry pan and sauté leeks, covered, until tender. Add potatoes, broth and cook until potatoes are soft. Mash potatoes slightly in soup. Add milk (cream, ½ and ½ or water) and season to taste. Heat but do not boil. Ladle into individual soup bowls, top with egg, bacon, parsley and serve.

A man calls his wife and says he is coming home for lunch, which is something he never does. When he reaches his house, he opens the front door only to find his naked wife sliding down the banister of the second story stairs.
"What in the world are you doing?" asks the stunned husband?"
"I'm warming up your lunch" replies the wife.

Five Onion Soup

½ pound scallions, diced
¾ pounds red onions, diced
¾ pounds yellow onions, diced
¾ pounds leeks, diced
¼ pounds fresh basil, chopped
¼ pounds shallots, chopped
1 teaspoon sugar
5 quarts demi glaze
¾ cups heavy cream
Salt and pepper, to taste
1 cups red wine
½ cups sherry, cooking
3 Tablespoons plus 1 Tablespoon olive oil (add more if necessary)
Very large yellow onions cooked and hollowed out to use as soup bowls

In a large fry pan, heat oil and butter and add onions, leeks basil and shallots. Sauté onions for 15 to 20 minutes or until onions are soft and translucent. Add 1 teaspoon sugar and continue to cook onions until they have turned a golden brown, adding a little more sugar if necessary to complete browning. Add demi glaze and cook for 5 minutes. Add cream, salt and pepper and continue cooking for 15 minutes. Place precooked yellow onion soup bowls on a serving plate and ladle soup into the bowls, top with Swiss or Gruyere cheese slices, and place under the broiler until cheese is brown and soup is hot. Sprinkle with chopped parsley and serve.

Note-- soup may also be served in onion soup bowls or hollowed out bread bowls. (1 pound sour dough bread rounds with tops removed)

An Italian, a Pollack and a Irishman are having lunch together as they do everyday. The Italian opens up his lunchbox and says.. if this is another balony sandwich I am going to kill myself, and it was. The Irishman opens his lunchbox and says if this a balony sandwich I am going to commit suicide, and it was a balony sandwich. The Pollack opens his lunchbox and says if this a balony sandwich, I am going to kill myself as well. And of course his sandwich is also balony. The three workers all commit suicide. A! the funeral, the wives are inconsolable. The Italian wife says, if I had only sent him a meatball sub, he would still be alive. The Irishman's wife says.. if I had only made him a corn beef sandwich, he might still be with me. The Pollack's wife said.. he made his own lunch!

Baked Onion Soup

Preheat broiler and preheat oven to 350 degrees
Serves 6 to 8

3 Tablespoon butter
1 Tablespoon olive oil
1½ pounds onions, sliced thin (Vidalia's make broth taste sweeter)
½ teaspoon sugar
3 Tablespoon flour
8 cups demi glaze veal or beef (may substitute equal parts of beef
    or chicken broth, beef consomme and beer)
1 cup white or red wine
½ teaspoon sage
2 bay leaves
6 to 8 slices of Swiss or Gruyere cheese,
3 to 4 tablespoons fresh grated parmesan cheese
6 to 8 thick sliced buttered and toasted French Baguettes

In a large sauce pan, heat oil and butter and add onions. Stir onions, coating them with the butter. Cover pan and sauté over medium heat, until onions are tender and translucent. Uncover pan, raise heat and add sugar. The sugar will help the onions brown. Continue to cook, about 7 minutes, or until onions have turned a deep golden brown. Lower heat and stir in flour, until flour and onions form a paste, adding more butter if flour does not make a paste with the onions. Continue to cook slowly, until flour turns a light brown, stirring constantly.

Heat broth and add 1 cup to flour onion mixture, using wooden spoon or wire whip to blend. Add rest of broth, wine, sage, bay leaf and simmer for 30 to 40 minutes. Soup may be made in a crock pot.

Note-- the more you reduce the soup and the more cheese you use, the saltier the broth will get. Adjust seasonings. If you are not serving immediately, cool, place soup in sealed container and refrigerate or freeze. Butter thick slices of French Baguettes and bake at 350 degrees, until toasted on both sides.

To serve
Ladle hot soup into onion soup bowls, or oven proof soup bowls. Place toasted baguette slices on top of soup. Top bread with parmesan, gruyere or Swiss cheeses and run under broiler until cheese melts and soup is hot. Place a serving dish under hot soup bowl and serve. Soup may also be served in precooked hollowed out yellow onions or 1 pound sour dough bread rounds with the tops removed.

Gazpacho Soup

2 cups tomato, peeled and coarsely chopped
1 cup colored pepper, coarsely chopped
1 cup cucumber, peeled and cubed
½ cup sweet Vidalia onions, finely chopped
Fresh parsley and /or chives, finely chopped
6 Tablespoons tarragon vinegar
3 Tablespoons olive oil
2 teaspoons salt
½ teaspoon fresh ground pepper
1 Tablespoon Worcestershire sauce
1 teaspoon Tabasco
4 cups tomato juice
Lemon juice, to taste
Green and black pitted olives, coarsely chopped

Assemble all ingredients in a large container and chill. When ready to serve, ladle mixture into individual serving bowls and decorate with toppings.

***Note*--** for a pretty presentation, use colored peppers as soup holders.

Topping
Sour cream, avocado slices, and lemon wedges.

Low Fat Cold Zucchini Soup

3 fresh zucchinis, remove only ½ the skin (for color) cut into large strips
10 cloves garlic, peeled
2 small onions
1 colored pepper
1 teaspoon salt, or to taste
Chicken stock, enough to cover ingredients to ¾ full
3 six ounce cans evaporated milk or an equal amount of ½ and ½

In a large pot, place zucchini, garlic, onions, colored pepper, and salt. Add chicken broth to cover ¾ of the ingredients. Cover and bring to boil. Reduce heat and simmer for 10 minutes. Remove from heat and allow mixture to cool. Place cooled mixture in a food processor, add evaporated milk and puree and refrigerate. When ready to serve, ladle into soup bowls and serve.

Hamburgers Sunnyside Up

Preheat grill
Serves 6

1½ pound ground round steak
1½ pound ground chuck steak
6 eggs, fried or poached
6 thick slices bacon, cooked crisp, reserve bacon fat
6 cheese slices (cheddar, monterey jack, havarti, American)
6 Kaiser or French Hamburger rolls, sliced
Salt, pepper and Worcestershire sauce
Condiments
Pam

Combine ground meats and make 6 patties. Place your thumb in the center of each patty, leaving an indentation. Lift grill lid and spray grates with Pam. Place burgers very close to flame. Sear meat and turn. Season and sprinkle with plenty of Worcestershire to create flame. When underside of patty has seared, flip hamburger to original side, season and return to other side. Top with cheese and close grill lid. When cheese is melted, remove meat to platter and cover with plastic wrap, until inside of meat has reached desired temperature.

Fry eggs in bacon reserved bacon grease, either sunny side up or down or make poached eggs with runny centers, and top burgers.
Place on buns (which may be toasted) add condiments and serve.

Note-- also delicious with sautéed mushrooms, grilled, sautéed, or raw onion slices, tomato slices, and Thousand Island dressing (see "NAUGHTY SAUCY")

What's the difference between football in the north and football in the south?
NORTH--College stadiums hold 20,000 people.
SOUTH--High school stadiums hold 20,000 people.
NORTH--Campus décor features statues of founding fathers
SOUTH--Campus décor features statues of Heisman Trophy winners
NORTH--One hour before game time, Campus parking opens.
SOUTH--Decorated RV's with school flags and mascots start arriving on Wednesday to begin the festivities. The truly faithful arrive Tuesday!

Lump Crab filled Avocado

Serves 4

1 pound jumbo lump blue crab meat (Costco has best price)
2 ripe avocados, peeled
Thousand Island dressing (see "NAUGHTY SAUCY")

Cut avocados the long way and remove the pit. Place on individual serving plates or large serving platter, fill with crab meat, top with dressing and serve.

A really old man goes to a whore house. The Madame takes one look at his age and decrepit body and says
"I am afraid; we can't do anything for you!"
He shows her a wad of big bills and she sends him down the hall to room 106.
It takes him forever to get his walker down the hall, but eventually he knocks on the door of room 106.
A gal in a beautiful blue negligee opens the door, takes one look and says "I don't' think I can do anything for you !!!!!!!!!!"
He shows her a wad of big bills and she changes her mind.
He undresses, shrinkage and shriveled are not strong enough adjectives to describe his penis.
She asks what she can do and he says:
"Snap your fingers"
And all of a sudden he grows 3 inches.
She snaps again and he is now 6 inches.
She snaps again and he is 9 inches. She realizes now that she has gone a little too far and asks if she can make it smaller again.
He tells her to pounds his heart and down he goes to 6 inches again.
He now suggests she get on top.
Snapping his fingers and beating his heart, he sings "If I were a rich man da de da de da de da de dee....."

Sandwiches

Peppered bacon, lettuce, tomato, sliced avocado, woked butterfly shrimp, Swiss cheese melted, mayonnaise, on toasted sour dough

Thick sliced crisp cooked peppered bacon, sliced tomato, poached or fried egg, avocado slices, mayonnaise, on lightly toasted Pepperidge Farm or Sara Lee toasting sandwich bread.

Turkey, cream cheese, cranberry spread, on cranberry bread or grilled sour dough bread

Sliced roasted turkey, coleslaw, thousand Island dressing on sliced seeded rye bread

Roasted turkey, coleslaw, bacon, corned beef, swiss cheese, melted, thousand island dressing on sliced seeded rye bread

Rare top round roast beef, coleslaw, thousand Island dressing, on sliced seeded rye bread.

Lean corned beef and pastrami, schmear of chopped liver, chicken fat (optional) coleslaw on thickly sliced seeded rye bread.

Sliced rotisserie roasted chicken, skin included, fresh basil leaves, toasted pine nuts, caponata (egg plant), **Fanny Farmer** (see "SKINNY DIPPING") on a long sour dough baguette, thickly sliced.

Monte Christo Smoked turkey, sliced ham, and havarti cheese, rolled together to make small bundles, flour dipped and beer battered (see "A LITTLE SOMETHING ON THE SIDE" **Beer Batter**) and deep fat fried in an electric fryer at 375 degrees until golden brown. Sprinkle with powdered sugar and top with fruit preserves.

Chicken salad and fried or poached egg placed on toasted and buttered English muffin.

Thin pizza dough, grilled until you see the black grill marks, roasted red and yellow pepper strips, goat cheese, spring green mix, and grilled chicken slices, and **balsamic dressing** (see "LETTUCE DRESS YOU")

Ahi Tuna seared rare (see **"Foreplay"**) on a lightly toasted, buttered bun, topped with Wasabi aioli (see "NAUGHTY SAUCY")

Wraps

1 package flour burritos
½ pound sliced mushrooms
1 small sweet onion, thinly sliced
Mexican grated cheese blend
Alfalfa sprouts
Grilled or rotisserie chicken, thinly sliced
Chipotle mayonnaise
4 Tablespoons of butter, divided

In a small skillet, melt 2 tablespoons of butter and sauté onions until well browned. Remove onions to a small plate and set aside until ready to assemble wrap.

Melt 2 tablespoons of butter in the same skillet and sauté the sliced mushrooms, until all moisture has evaporated and mushrooms have lightly browned.

Cut one of the burritos in half. Have stove top burner heated on low temperature. Place burrito half directly on the heated stove top burner and warm bottom of burrito half, while you spread chipotle mayonnaise evenly on the side not on the heat. Layer grated cheese over mayonnaise. Take remaining ingredients, onions, mushrooms, chicken and alfalfa sprouts and place down the center section, making the layer thin enough to fold up the bottom edge of the burrito and fold in the sides so they over lap. Turn the burrito to the uncooked side and grill till warmed and lightly browned. Continue in this fashion until all the ingredients have been used up. Cooked burrito halves may be wrapped in foil and kept warm in an oven heated to 200 degrees, until ready to serve, or wrapped and placed in a small cooler to keep warm.

***Note*--** Chicken may be replaced with sautéed or grilled steak, sautéed onions, sautéed mushrooms, and sautéed colored pepper strips. Any type of grated or crumbled cheese, crumbled crisp bacon, and chopped tomatoes may be used. Fill burrito with grilled chicken, fresh grated parmesan cheese, romaine lettuce, bottled Caesar salad dressing fold and wrap.

a fare to remember

A man calls up his friend the farmer "Do you still want to sell that mare of yours?
"Oh, yes "says the farmer.
"Well I think I may have a buyer", says the friend and asks him,
"Can I bring him around Saturday morning and show him the horse?"
"That would be wonderful" the farmer answered.
The friend says "There is one thing I would like to mention about the potential buyer. He is a midget with a hair lip"!
So Saturday morning arrives and the friend brings the midget to see the farmer's mare.
"Oh" says the midget, "thath a vewy nith horth. Do you think you could lift me up so thad I could look at her gums?"
So the farmer picks the midget up and shows him the horse's gums.
"Her gums are wewy pink" says the midget "that's a wewy good sign".
The farmer puts the midget down and the midget walks around, studying the horse.
The midget turns to the farmer and says,
"Do you think you could lift me up so thad I could look in her eyeths?
So the farmer obliges and the midget says, "Oh, her eyeths are clear, thad's great, I think I am going to wove this horth".
The farmer puts him down and the midget continues to circle the mare. Finally he says to the farmer, "could you just pick me up so thad I could look into her ears"?
Now the farmer is getting really annoyed. The midget might be small but he is really heavy, however, he really wants to sell the horse, so he picks him up again.
The midget looks into the horse's ears and exclaims "Oh there are no bugths. He must be really healthy".
The farmer puts the midget down.
The midget asks "Can I see her Twat"?
The frustrated farmer grabs the midget and shoves him up the horse's butt.
The midget shakes himself off and says,
"I guess I should rephrase that, can I see her run !!!!!!!!"

wild chicks

Amazing Chicken Cacciatore

Serves 6

3 pounds frying chicken pieces, bone in (breasts, thighs, legs, wings)
3 Tablespoons butter
1 Tablespoon olive oil
1 clove garlic, finely chopped (or ½ teaspoon jarred chopped garlic)
2 cans whole pimentos, drained and cut into 1 inch squares
½ teaspoon oregano
¼ teaspoon pepper
1½ teaspoons salt
1 Tablespoon flour
3 Tablespoons sherry
½ cup tomato juice (not V-8 juice)
½ fresh sliced mushrooms
2 Tablespoons butter

In a small fry pan, sauté mushrooms in 2 tablespoons butter and set aside.

In a large fry pan, heat 3 tablespoons butter and oil. Add chicken and brown on all sides over moderate heat. Add garlic and brown. Add rest of ingredients, except mushrooms. Cover skillet and simmer for 1 hour. If chicken appears dry, add additional tomato juice or wine. Turn chicken pieces several times during the simmering. When chicken is tender, add the mushrooms. Cover again and continue cooking for 5 minutes. If there is too much liquid, uncover and cook for a few more minutes. Place chicken on serving platter or individual dishes, top with remaining ingredients in the pan, and spoon sauce on top.

Sauce
2 Tablespoons butter
1 medium onion, cut into 1 inch squares
1 small colored pepper (red, yellow, orange, or green), cut into ½ inch squares
1 teaspoon salt
½ teaspoon black pepper
2 Tablespoons fresh grated parmesan cheese
1 cup canned or fresh peeled tomatoes
2 Tablespoons finely cut parsley

Heat butter until hot; add onions and peppers, and sauté 5 minutes. Crush tomatoes, by hand, until you have medium sized pieces. Simmer, uncovered, for about 15 minutes or until mixture is quite thick.

Chicken Crepes

Preheat oven to 375 degrees
Serves 10

Crepe Batter
3 eggs
1 cup milk
2 Tablespoons butter, melted and cooled
½ teaspoon salt
Dash of cayenne pepper
⅛ teaspoon nutmeg
½ cup flour, sifted

Beat eggs with milk, butter and seasoning. Gradually add flour, beating until smooth. Refrigerate covered for 2 hours or more.

Filling
4 Tablespoons butter
2 onions, chopped
2 cups (½ pound) mushrooms, thinly sliced
¼ cup (½ of 10-ounce package) cooked spinach, drained and chopped
2 cups cooked chicken, coarsely chopped
4 Tablespoons sour cream
2 Tablespoons sherry
½ teaspoon salt
Dash of cayenne

Heat butter in large skillet. Sauté onions until soft and golden. Add mushrooms and cook for 4 minutes, stirring occasionally. Stir in spinach, chicken, sour cream, sherry, salt and cayenne. Remove from heat and refrigerate until needed.

Sauce
4 Tablespoons butter
4 Tablespoons flour
2 cups chicken broth
1 cup milk
½ cup parmesan cheese, grated
½ cup Swiss or Gruyere cheese, grated
Salt to taste
Dash of cayenne
⅛ teaspoon saffron (optional)
½ cup sherry

continued

Melt butter. Blend in flour until smooth. Gradually stir in broth and mix. Cook over low heat, stirring constantly until smooth. Add grated cheese and seasoning. Stir over low heat until cheese is melted. Remove from heat and add sherry. Cool. Pack in container and freeze.

Crepes
Heat a 6" skillet over medium heat for 2 to 3 minutes. Pan will be ready, when a drop of oil sizzles when added. Swirl 1 tablespoon of vegetable oil in pan and pour out any excess. Pour in about 2 tablespoons of batter, rotating pan quickly to spread batter evenly over bottom. Cook over medium heat until lightly browned on one side. Turn and brown the other side lightly. Remove to parchment paper. Repeat process until batter is used.

Place 2 tablespoons of filling in center of each crepe. Flap one side of crepe over filling. Fold ends in and roll up. Place seam side down on flat surface and chill in freezer for one hour. Remove to refrigerator or pack in a container with freezer paper between layers and freeze.

Serving Day
Remove crepes from refrigerator or, if frozen, thaw crepes at room temperature for one hour or more. Heat sauce in a sauce pan over very low heat, stirring frequently. Place crepes on a greased, shallow baking dish, seam side down, leaving space between crepes. Place 1 tablespoon of sauce on top of each crepe. Bake at 375 degrees for 25 minutes until lightly browned. Pour on more sauce and bake another 20 to 25 minutes, then broil until nicely brown. Serve with remaining hot sauce.

Alternate Preparation for Serving Day
Thaw crepes at room temperature for 1 hour or more. Place on greased broiler pan. Top with one tablespoon of heated sauce. Broil 3 to 4" from heat for about 15 minutes, until nicely browned. Serve with remaining hot sauce.

To serve without freezing, bake as directed, for 20 minutes. Top with more sauce and bake an additional 10 minutes or broil for about 10 to 12 minutes, until nicely browned.

Bumper Sticker
"Food has replaced SEX in my life.
Now I can't even get into my own pants"!!!

Chicken Jubilee

Preheat oven 325 degrees

Chicken breasts, thighs, and legs, with bones and skin
2 teaspoons salt
½ cup butter, melted
¼ teaspoon pepper
1 cup water
½ cup raisins
½ cup brown sugar
1 teaspoon garlic salt
2 medium onions sliced
12 ounces chili sauce
1 Tablespoon Worcestershire sauce
1 16 ounce can Bing cherries, pitted and drained (or fresh cherries)
1 cup white wine

Place chicken in shallow roasting pan, skin side up, single layer. Season and dribble with butter. Broil under medium flame or grill until brown.

Combine remaining ingredients, except for cherries and wine. Mix well and pour over chicken. Cover with foil and bake 325 for 45 minutes. Remove foil and add wine and cherries   Continue baking, uncovered for an additional 15 minutes.

Note-- This dish tastes best with chicken pieces on the bone with skin. Any left over sauce can be frozen for future use. This dish can be made ahead and frozen.

A man goes to a whore house but the Madame says she has no more rooms.
He says he doesn't care, just give him a woman and he'll go up on the roof top.
Now a drunk is walking by when the couple on the roof gets carried away and falls off the roof.
The drunk goes inside and says to the Madame, "I think your sign just fell over"!

Chicken Marsala

Preheat oven to 350 degrees

8 Tablespoons butter
¼ cup flour
1 teaspoon salt
⅛ teaspoon pepper
½ teaspoon fresh chopped chives
1 teaspoon gravy master
¾ cup dry white wine (Marsala)
1 can Swanson beef broth
½ to 1 lb. mushrooms
2 cups sliced onions
½ clove garlic

Place in plastic baggie
½ cup flour
1 ½ teaspoon salt
¼ cup paprika

Melt 4 tablespoons of butter and add 1 tablespoon of olive oil. Sauté chicken quickly and remove from pan. Set aside. Add 4 tablespoons butter to pan and sauté onions and garlic. In a separate pan sauté mushrooms and set aside.

Add ¼ cup seasoned flour, ¾ cup Marsala and 1 cup Swanson beef broth, salt and pepper, Gravy Master, chives and tarragon. Flatten breasts, butter and fill with sun-dried tomatoes, shitake mushrooms, ricotta cheese and herbs; maybe even spinach leaves, cooked. Roll in a heavy crust with paprika. Brown. Add Marsala sauce. Can use flour, eggs and bread crumbs. Bake at 350 degrees.

A father tells his teenage son that if he ever drinks too much, not to drive, but to call him any time of day or night and no matter where he is, the Dad will come and get him and he won't get into any trouble.
So one night, the phone rings and the Dad is awakened out of a sound sleep by the ringing of the phone. He picks up the reciever only to hear his son say "Dad, I'm drunk!" The father immediately says" Son, stay right where you are. I'll be right there to get you. Where are you?" asks the Dad. "I'm in the living room" answers the son.

Chicken Mozzarella

Preheat oven to 350 degrees
Serves 6

6 chicken breast halves, skinned and boned
Salt and pepper, to taste
½ cup butter, divided, at room temperature
8 ounces whole milk mozzarella, cut lengthwise into 6 sticks
½ cup all-purpose flour
2 eggs, beaten
1 cup fine dry bread crumbs
1 teaspoon dried marjoram
½ teaspoon dried thyme
½ cup Sauvignon Blanc or other dry white wine
2 tablespoons finely chopped fresh parsley

Place boneless chicken breasts between 2 sheets of plastic wrap. Flatten to ¼" thickness, using a veal pounder, mallet, or rolling pin. Pound, don't roll, being careful to leave chicken fillet in one piece.

Spread chicken filets with ½ of the softened butter, reserving the rest of the butter for the sauce. Top each chicken breast with a stick of mozzarella. Sprinkle with salt and pepper. Fold sides of chicken over cheese and roll up, tucking in ends. Secure rolls with wooden toothpicks. Dredge rolls in flour, dip in egg, and coat with bread crumbs. Dip ends into egg mixture and reseal with bread crumbs. Place seam side down in a buttered 13 x 9 x 2" baking dish.

Melt remaining ¼ cup butter. Combine herbs and parsley and pour butter mixture over breasts. Bake uncovered at 350 degrees for 20 minutes. Remove from oven and pour wine over chicken rolls and baste with wine, including herbed butter in the bottom of the pan. Return to oven and bake, uncovered. Continue baking for 15 minutes, basting every 5 minutes and again before serving. Reserve any extra wine gravy to serve over white and wild rice. Remove toothpicks before serving.

For variety, instead of marjoram, use: 1 teaspoon oregano, ½ teaspoon rosemary, and ¼ cup plus 2 tablespoons butter in sauce.

Serve with Uncle Ben's White and Wild Rice and a green vegetable.

Chicken Picatta

Serves 4

4 chicken breasts, skinned, boned, and cut into medallions
½ cup flour
1½ teaspoons salt
¼ teaspoon freshly ground pepper
Paprika
¼ cup butter for each pan of chicken
1 Tablespoon olive oil for each pan of chicken
4 Tablespoons dry Madeira wine for each pan of chicken
1½ teaspoon fresh lemon juice, for each pan of chicken
Lemon slices, cut very thin
4 Tablespoons capers (optional) for each pan of chicken
¼ cup minced fresh parsley (optional garnish)

Note-- The number of batches depends on the size of the pan you use and how many chicken medallions you are cooking. Skinless chicken breasts, pounded thin, may be used instead of medallions.

Combine flour, salt, pepper and paprika in plastic bag. Add a few chicken fingers at a time (or whole breasts) and coat well. Shake off excess.

Melt butter and 1 tablespoon olive oil, in large skillet, preferably electric frying pan set at 375 degrees and heat until bubbling. Add some of the floured chicken fingers and brown for 2 to 3 minutes on each side. Do not crowd the pan as you want plenty of chicken drippings for gravy.

Remove cooked chicken medallions to a side plate while you make the gravy. You should have about 2 tablespoons of oil plus drippings left in pan. If you have more, drain off all but 2 tablespoons. Add about four paper thin lemon slices and 2 tablespoons of capers (or to taste) to hot pan and sauté. With eyes averted, add 1 ½ tablespoons lemon juice and ¼ cup Madeira wine, into drippings, scraping bottom of skillet to loosen any browned bits. Heat briefly and return cooked chicken medallions to pan, coating each piece with gravy. Remove chicken and place in an oven-proof dish. Cover with plastic wrap, and set aside while you make the other batches of chicken.

Repeat process until all the chicken is cooked. Serve immediately with rice. Chicken can be topped with chopped parsley (optional).
Chicken is best served immediately, but it can easily be made ahead and reheated, covered, in preheated oven at 350 degrees or microwave. Chicken dish may be made ahead of time and reheated Chicken may also be frozen. Sprinkle with minced parsley, optional.

Coq Au Vin (Chicken in Red Wine)

Serves 4 to 6

5 strips bacon
5½ Tablespoons butter, divided
1½ Tablespoons olive oil
3 lbs frying chicken, breasts, wings, thighs, and drum sticks
2 cans beef bouillon (or chicken demi glaze)
½ lb sliced mushrooms, sautéed
24 white onions (brown braised)
Flour
Parsley springs
¼ cup cognac
3 cups red wine (burgundy, Beaujolais, Chianti)
Salt & Pepper
½ Tablespoon tomato paste
2 cloves mashed garlic
¼ teaspoon thyme
1 bay leaf

In a large skillet, melt 1 tablespoon butter and sauté bacon. Remove to a side dish, reserving bacon grease. Using paper towels, pat chicken pieces until dry. Brown chicken pieces in remaining hot bacon grease until chicken is browned on all sides. Season chicken with a little salt and pepper, return cooked bacon to the pan, cover and cook slowly for about 10 minutes, turning the chicken pieces once. Uncover and pour in cognac. Avert your face and light cognac with a long match. Shake skillet back and forth until flames subside. Pour wine into skillet and add enough bouillon to cover chicken. Stir in paste, garlic and herbs (thyme and bay leaf). .

In a separate fry pan, heat 1½ tablespoon butter and 1½ tablespoons olive oil, until hot and bubbly. When foam subsides, add 24 small white peeled onion creamers, rolling them so that they will brown. Sauté onions until well browned, about 10 minutes. Add to chicken, cover and simmer for 30 to 40 minutes, or until chicken is tender.

In a small fry pan, heat 2 tablespoons of butter and sauté mushrooms for 4 to 5 minutes. Add to chicken.

To make gravy
Simmer chicken cooking liquid on low heat. Skim off fat. Raise heat and boil liquid rapidly, reducing liquid to 2 ½ cups. Pour liquid into a container with a lid and add 3 tablespoons flour. With lid on, shake until mixture is smooth. Place liquid in a food processor, add salt, pepper, and 2 tablespoons of soft butter. Pulse until sauce is thick enough to coat a spoon. Arrange mushroom and onions around chicken in casserole. Baste with warmed sauce and serve.

Fried Chicken – Italian Style

Chicken pieces - thighs, breasts, wings, legs, and drums
1 cup flour
1 Tablespoon salt
½ teaspoon pepper
Paprika
Garlic salt
Oil for frying

Dip pieces of chicken in flour seasoned with salt, pepper, paprika, and garlic salt. Place above ingredients in a plastic bag. Add chicken to coat; remove from plastic bag and shake off excess flour. Place on large cookie sheet.

Mix together
2 Tablespoons lemon juice
¼ cup olive oil
Salt & pepper
2 bay leaves
Dash of oregano

Pour over chicken, or pat on with pastry brush. Let stand one hour or longer in refrigerator.

Sprinkle chicken with fresh grated Parmesan and Romano cheeses.

Deep fry each batch of chicken in oil heated to 375 degrees for approximately 5 to 7 minutes for or until chicken pieces turn golden brown. Sprinkle extra paprika on chicken before frying to attain quicker browning. .For southern fried chicken, use bacon fat.

The new KFC Bucket called "The Hillary Pack" has:

2 big thighs
2 small breasts
2 left wings

Poached Chicken

Chicken fryer pieces, boneless, or with bones
Rich chicken stock, or canned chicken broth, enough to cover
    chicken pieces
1 cup dry white wine or sauterne
1 bunch scallions, with green tops
Celery leafy tops
Baby carrots
Salt and pepper
Bay leaves (a few)
1 pound green beans (added later)

In a large stock pot or roasting pan,, add chicken pieces that have been salt and peppered, wine, bay leaves, carrots, scallions, and celery tops. Poach over very low heat, just high enough so that chicken poaches and does not simmer, for about 30 minutes Add green beans and poach an additional 10 minutes, or until chicken juices run clear when cut and the chicken is not pink inside.

If preparing whole chickens, rather than parts, present the chicken whole and carve into slices. If serving the chicken cold, top with jellied stock and garnish with vegetables. Other vegetables, such as pearl onions or peeled and cubed turnips may be used.

Note-- This recipe is great for dieters. The chicken in the juices may be stored in baggies and frozen, to be used at another time as cooked chicken, either for sandwiches or salads, or for soups.

One hot summer day a husband decides to mow the yard naked. His wife is horrified "Don't do that" she cries "they'll think I married you for your money."

Roast Turkey - The Old Fashioned Way

Preheat oven to 325 degrees

Allow 1 pound of turkey per person and extra for leftovers.

To prepare turkey
Fresh is better than frozen, and it will take a little less time to cook. Remove neck package and discard livers. In heavy pot, place neck and giblets, scallions, raw carrot and celery stick, including leafy part. Cover with chicken broth or water and chicken bouillon cubes or granules. Simmer several hours. Drain. Use liquid and giblets for gravy.

Wash turkey cavities and drain. Using two different prepared dressings loosely fill turkey cavities. Sew flap to bird or secure with toothpicks to keep stuffing sealed at small end. You do not have to secure the large end, but you don't want the stuffing to fall out. Using salt, pepper, and paprika, season top and bottom of turkey... Place on rack in roasting pan, breast side up.

Melt a stick of butter and gradually pour over all turkey surfaces. Place meat thermometer in the plumpest part of the breast. Do not use self-popping thermometer that may already be in the breast. Turkey is done when temperature reaches 165 degrees.

Roast bird for 20 minutes and baste. Tent the turkey loosely with aluminum foil. Return to oven and repeat basting every 20 to 30 minutes until one hour before the bird is done. Remove foil tent so that the skin can brown. Continue to baste until turkey is done. Allow to sit 20 minutes before carving.

Gravy
Remove bird from roaster. Place on carving board and cover with foil tent. Drain off all fat. Add turkey broth and scrape all drippings from bottom and sides of pan.

In a small glass jar, add some flour and water or cooled chicken broth and shake, dissolving all lumps. Add to roaster, stirring constantly to keep smooth. Add salt, pepper, poultry seasoning, and Gravy Master, to taste. More diluted flour or cornstarch can be used if thicker gravy is desired. Do not allow to boil. Extra gravy may be frozen for later use.

Turkey Notes
When using meat thermometer, do not allow any part to touch turkey bones.

The best way to make gravy is to put roasting pan with drippings into the freezer after the cooked bird has been removed. Allow fat to harden. Peel off and discard or use as a gravy separator. Turkey can be wrapped in plastic wrap after it is roasted and stored in an insulated container for two hours prior to serving. If you only have one oven, this will free it up to cook other dishes. Freeze any leftover gravy for later use or for turkey soup.

CHRISTMAS CAROLS for PERSONALTY DISORDERS

SCHIZOPHRENIA---"Do you hear what I hear????"
MULTIPLE PERSONALITY---"We three Queens disoriented are."
NARCISSISTIC---Hark the Herald Angels sing about ME"
MANIC---Deck the halls and the walls and the house and the Streets and the stores and office and town and Cars and busses and trucks and trees and fire Hydrants and .....
PASSIVE-AGGRESSIVE PERSONALITY---"On the first day Day of Christmas my true love gave to me" (and then he took it all away)
PARANOID--"Santa Claus is coming to get me."
DEPRESSION--"Silent night, all is dark, all is flat, all is lonely."
BORDERLINE PERSONALITY---"You better watch out, I'm gonna cry, I'm gonna pout, maybe I'll tell you why!"
OBSESSIVE COMPULSIVE---
  Jingle Bells, Jingle bells, Jingle bells,
  Jingle bells, Jingle bells, Jingle bells
  Jingle bells, Jingle bells, Jingle bells,
  Jingle bells, Jingle bells, Jingle bells

Spanish Chicken with Apricots

Preheat oven to 350 degrees
Serves 10 plus

2½ pounds chicken, sectioned (legs, thighs, breasts and wings)
1 head of garlic, peeled and finely pureed
¼ cup dried oregano
Coarse salt and freshly ground pepper, to taste
½ cup red wine vinegar
½ cup olive oil
1 cup dried apricots
½ cup capers with a bit of juice
6 bay leaves
1 cup brown sugar
1 cup white wine
¼ cup Italian parsley or fresh coriander, finely chopped

In a large bowl, combine chicken pieces (skin on), garlic, oregano, pepper and coarse salt to taste, vinegar, olive oil, apricots, capers and juice, and bay leaves. Cover and marinate overnight in refrigerator.

Arrange chicken in a single layer in one or two large, shallow baking pans and spoon marinade evenly over chicken. Sprinkle chicken pieces with brown sugar and pour white wine around them.

Bake for 50 minutes to 1 hour, basting frequently with pan juices. Chicken is done when thigh pieces, pricked with a fork at their thickest, yield clear yellow (rather than pink) juice.

With a slotted spoon, transfer chicken, apricots, and capers to a serving platter. Moisten with a few spoonfuls of pan juices and sprinkle generously with parsley or cilantro. Pass remaining pan juices in a sauceboat.

To serve chicken cold, cool to room temperature in cooking juices before transferring to a serving platter. If chicken has been covered and refrigerated, allow it to return to room temperature before serving. Spoon some of the reserved juice over chicken.

Note-- this is also delicious with olives, prunes, or other dried fruit.

Stir-Fried Almond Chicken

Preheat oven 300 degrees
Serves 4

2 pounds chicken breasts, skinless, boneless cut into 1 inch cubes
1 egg white
1 can water chestnuts, chopped
4 stalks celery, chopped
4 large Shitake dried mushrooms, prepared and quartered
2 Tablespoons corn starch
1 Tablespoon dry sherry
1½ teaspoons salt
1 teaspoon M.S.G (accent) optional
½ cup water
½ cup toasted almonds
5 Tablespoons oil
Butter

Line small baking pan with aluminum foil and add nuts. Top with pats of butter or spray butter. Bake until lightly browned.

Blend together salt, egg white, sherry, and corn starch. Stir in chicken until all cubes are coated.

Prepare mushrooms by covering them with hot water and letting them soak until softened.

In wok, heat 2 tablespoons oil. When hot, add mushrooms, celery, water chestnuts, ½ teaspoon salt, and MSG. Stir-fry for 2 to 3 minutes. Remove from pan and set aside.

In wok, heat 3 tablespoons oil until very hot. Stir-fry chicken in single layer, allowing space between chicken cubes, until they turn white. Remove from pan and set aside until all chicken has been cooked. Add vegetable mixture to chicken and return to wok, stir-frying for one minute. Add 1/3 cup of water, bring to boil and serve.

Top with toasted almonds.   Serve over rice.

Rice- use 2 cups rice to 3 cups water. For drier rice, reduce water to 2½ cups water. Rinse rice to remove starch. Turn burner on high heat and boil water. Add 2 tablespoons butter to water. Once water has boiled, remove pot from burner, leave top off for 2 minutes, reduce burner to low heat, add rice, cover and cook with *lid on* for 25 minutes.

Oriental Walnut Chicken

Serves 4

Marinade
1 Tablespoon vegetable oil
2 teaspoons soy sauce
1 teaspoon cornstarch
4 chicken breast halves, skinned, boned, and cut into 1" pieces

Broth mixture
½ cup chicken broth
1 Tablespoon soy sauce
½ teaspoon ground ginger
½ teaspoon cayenne pepper
¼ cup vegetable oil for frying
1 sweet red pepper, cut into 1" pieces
1 medium onion, cut into 1" pieces
1 clove garlic, minced
½ pound broccoli, cut into 1" pieces
½ cup chopped walnuts or cashews
Hot cooked rice

Combine 1 tablespoon oil, 2 teaspoons soy sauce, and 1 teaspoon cornstarch; stir well. Add chicken; cover and marinate in refrigerator for 30 minutes.

Combine broth, ginger, 1 tablespoon soy sauce, and 2 teaspoons cornstarch; cayenne pepper and stir well.

Pour remaining ¼ cup oil in preheated wok. Stir fry coated chicken pieces in small batches until chicken is cooked. Remove from pan and set aside.

Add sweet red pepper, onion, garlic and stir-fry 1 minute. Add broccoli and stir fry 1 minute. Return chicken to wok and stir gently.

Add broth mixture; cook until thickened, stirring constantly. Stir in nuts. Serve over wild and white rice.

Suggestion
Add yellow pepper for more color and slightly increase soy sauce or use dark soy sauce.

in the boeuf

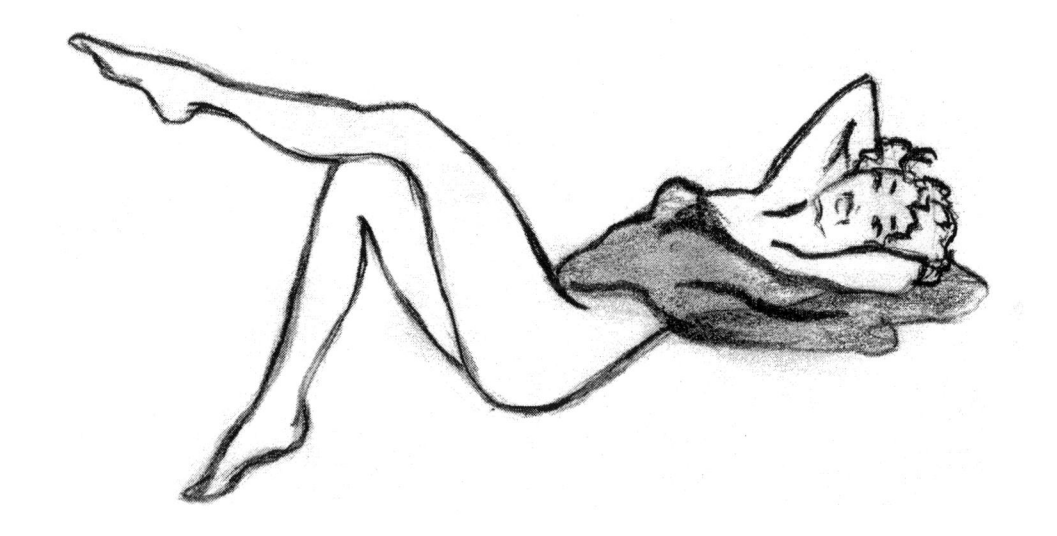

Chili with Filo

Preheat oven 375 degrees
Serves 4 to 6

2 pounds ground beef or turkey
1 small or medium onion, chopped
1 large can crushed tomatoes
2 (16 ounce) cans kidney beans, drained (optional)
3 Tablespoons chili powder
3 Tablespoons cumin seed (optional)
1 box frozen Filo sheets (2 per serving)
Butter, melted

Optional toppings
Pickled Jalapeño pepper rings, chopped onion, chopped tomatoes, sour cream, avocado, grated Mexican cheese, iceberg lettuce.

Brown beef (or turkey) and pour off remaining fat. Add crushed tomatoes, beans, chili powder, and cumin. Cover and simmer for approximately 45 minutes. Pour into individual oven-proof bowls and top with grated cheese.

Brush 2 Filo sheets per bowl with melted butter. Fold 1 sheet in half and in half again. Place over bowl. Ball up 2nd buttered sheet and place on top.

Bake at 375 degrees until brown, 10 to 15 minutes.

***Note*--** Chili can be made several days ahead and refrigerated. On serving day, heat chili before pouring into oven-proof bowls.

**Have you seen the newest Jewish-American Horror movie?
It's titled "Debbie Does Dishes"**

New York Sweet Chili

Preheat electric fry pan to 400 degrees
Serves 6 to 8

2 medium onions, chopped
2 stalks celery, diced
2 Tablespoons oil
2 pounds ground beef (use mix of ground chuck and ground round)
½ cup canned mushrooms
2 (8-ounce) cans stewed tomatoes
2 (10-ounce) cans tomato soup
1 cup boiling water
2 Tablespoons chili powder
1 Tablespoon sugar
½ + teaspoon salt
2 cans (4 cups) red kidney beans (optional)

Optional toppings
Grated cheeses, cheddar, monetary jack, Mexican or pizza blend, tomatoes, marinated jalapeno rings, chopped onions, chopped scallions, green tops included, chopped iceberg lettuce, black sliced olives, and corn chips.

Heat electric frying pan to 400 degrees. Add oil and sauté onions until translucent. Add celery and sauté until it softens. Add meat and brown. Drain and discard fat. Add remaining ingredients, cover, and simmer until all flavors are melded, about 45 minutes.

Serve in bowls and top with your choice of assorted toppings, or fill scooped out bread rounds and use as container for chili.

To serve as a salad, use iceberg lettuce and top as above, using the chili as the salad dressing, and the corn chips as crunch.

What are the three words a woman never wants to hear
when she is making love????
"HONEY I'M HOME"

Day Ahead Classic Brisket

Preheat oven to 325 degrees
Makes 10 servings

1 7-10 pound whole beef brisket
1 bottle 12 ounce Heinz Chili Sauce
1 envelope Lipton's Onion Soup mix
1 12-ounce Coca-Cola
Heavy duty aluminum foil
Baby carrots, cooked (optional)

Up to Five Days before Serving
Crisscross two sheets of heavy-duty aluminum foil in roasting pan, long enough to encase brisket. Place brisket fat side up, in middle of foil. The brisket can be taken directly from refrigerator; it does not have to be at room temperature.

Pour the chili sauce, onion-soup mix, and cola into a bowl and mix. (Don't be tempted to taste this; it's awful!) Pour the mixture over the brisket, lifting the brisket to let some of the liquid spread underneath it.

Seal foil and roast until fork-tender (about 2 hours). Uncover foil. The meat should be tender but still give a slight tug as you pull fork out. If it is not fork-tender, cover and return to oven, checking at 15-minute intervals. When brisket is done, remove from oven and cool. Pour cooled sauce into a container and refrigerate. Re-seal foil around brisket and place in refrigerator overnight. Once refrigerated, the roasted brisket and cold gravy can remain there 3 to 5 days before slicing, reheating and serving.

Serving Day Preheat oven to 350 degrees.
Trim off all visible fat from the cold brisket. Turn meat over and place on a cutting board. You should be looking at the lean side of the brisket. Look for the grain (the muscle line of the brisket indicated by lines on the meat).

With a sharp knife, slice the brisket on the bias (against the grain). If the slice appears stringy, you're slicing the wrong way. Return slices to foil.

Remove the gravy from the refrigerator. Discard fat. Heat the gravy and pour over brisket slices.

Optional At this point, add cooked baby carrots.

Seal foil. Bake brisket for 1 hour at 350 degrees. Best served with potato pancakes; see ("A LITTLE SOMETHING ON THE SIDE.")

Do Ahead Roast Beef

Preheat oven to 375 degrees

Rib roast, 5 pounds or more, preferably the first 3 to 4 ribs cut full
Salt & pepper
Garlic powder
Worcestershire sauce
Paprika
2 large yellow onions, sliced thick

Remove roast from refrigerator and allow it to reach room temperature: Season with above condiments. In bottom of roasting pan, layer ½ of the onion rounds. Place roast in pan and top with remaining onions. Use toothpicks to secure onions to meat.

Bake roast, fat side up, for 1 hour. Turn oven off. Keep oven door closed at least 4 hours or longer.

35 minutes before serving, turn oven on to 375 degrees. If desired, door can now be opened to add pre-cooked potatoes and/or carrots, rolling them in the drippings. Insert meat thermometer. Bake for an additional 35 to 40 minutes until thermometer reaches desired temperature. Remove from oven and allow to rest before slicing. Serve with Au Jus.

Frozen Boneless Rib Roast

Preheat grill very hot and oven to 450 degrees
Serves 3 to 4

3 pounds rib roast, boneless, frozen
2 onions, sliced
Worcestershire garlic salt, pepper and paprika
Onions, sliced

Unwrap frozen roast, place in a baggie and seal. Soak baggie in ice water, but do not allow water to seep in. Allow to defrost slightly. Pam grill grates and place meat close to heat and onions not as close to the flame. Sear meat heavily on all sides, seasoning as you turn roast. When meat thermometer will go into the roast, place meat and onions in a roasting pan and bake at 450 degrees until thermometer registers 120 degrees. Reduce temperature to 350 and continue to roast until thermometer registers 130 for medium rare. Allow to rest before slicing. Serve with au jus.

Grilled Sirloin Steak

Serves 6

3 pounds sirloin steak cut 1¾ to 2 inches thick (increase pounds if sirloin is not boneless)
1 cup red wine vinegar
½ cup soy sauce
½ cup olive oil
Worcestershire sauce, salt, and pepper

Marinate steak in oil, soy, and vinegar for no longer than 2 hours. Drain. Place steak on very hot grill that has been sprayed with Pam. Sear hard on high for 10 minutes. Turn and season with salt, pepper, and. Worcestershire after 5 minutes of grilling, flip steak to unseasoned side and season with salt, pepper, and Worcestershire sauce. Flip steak back to the other side and continue cooking until medium rare. When steak feels firm to the finger touch, it is usually done. With a sharp knife, test the meat by slicing into the thickest part. If steak is not pink enough, return to the grill and cook with grill lid closed for a few additional minutes until it is done.

Two Mid-Western spinsters away from home for the first time are on vacation in New York City. They visit the Central Park Zoo and become fascinated with the monkey House. They find themselves in front of the Gorilla cage,
The biggest, meanest Gorilla becomes very agitated. The spinsters taunt him. All of a sudden, with tremendous strength, the gorilla spreads the cage bars apart and pulls one of the spinsters into the cage.
He rapes and ravages her. The ambulance rushes her away before her friend can find out what Hospital they are going to take her. Her friend searches every Hospital and finally finds the patient. She rushes to her friend's bed side where she finds her bandaged from head to toe, in traction, tears flowing down her mummy wrapped face.
"I am so sorry "says her friend.
"I know, wails her bandaged friend, he didn't call!! He didn't write"!!!!!!

Individual Beef Wellington

Preheat oven to 400 degrees

4 beef filets, ½ pound each (without bacon)
Butter
Worcestershire sauce
Salt and pepper

Sear filets in butter in a heavy skillet, until lightly browned. Turn and season with Worcestershire sauce, salt, and pepper. Continue cooking until desired doneness is achieved.

Note-- Filets will not continue to cook when baked in pastry. (See "Helps" for determining rare, medium or well-done.)

Refrigerate for 2 hours or flash freeze to stop the meat from continuing to cook.

Pastry Filling
⅛ cup minced shallots
⅛ cup butter
½ pound mushrooms, very finely diced
¼ teaspoon salt
Dash of pepper
1¼ ounces of goose liver pate (or to taste)
1 box frozen puff pastry sheets

Cook shallots for 2 minutes in butter in large skillet over medium heat. Add mushrooms, salt and pepper. Cook stirring occasionally until all moisture disappears, approximately 7 to 8 minutes.

Stir in goose liver pate. Taste and adjust seasonings. Cool.

Pastry for Six individual Beef Wellingtons

Egg Wash 1 egg yolk + 1 tablespoon water, or one whole egg

Defrost frozen puff pastry; turn out on lightly floured surface and roll with lightly floured rolling pin. Make four 9 x 6 rectangles; reserve some pastry for decorations. Fill the center of each pastry rectangle, with ¼ of pastry filling.

continued

Place sautéed filets on top of filling. Brush edges of pastry with egg. Encase filet by bringing one side of pastry up to cover the filet. Then lift and bring the opposite side up and over. Pinch all ends using additional egg to firmly seal all edges.

Pick up filet with both hands and place on a lightly greased cookie sheet with seam-side down. Roll pastry trimmings; cut designs. Moisten with egg mixture and arrange on top. Continue in this manner, until all the filets have been wrapped in pastry.

At this point, you may wrap individual filets in plastic wrap and put into freezer bags. Refrigerate or freeze. If you do, let stand at room temperature for 20 minutes before baking. Either way, just before baking, beat egg yolk with 1 tablespoon water and brush it all over pastry and trimmings.

Bake at 400 degrees for 18 to 20 minutes. Pastry should be golden brown.

Serve with a warm Bordelaise, Brown, or Béarnaise sauce (see "NAUGHTY SAUCY") Garnish with sautéed, or stuffed mushrooms, carrot curls, and parsley sprigs. For a very special meal, serve tomato baskets filled with cauliflower and broccoli florets. (See "A LITTLE SOMETHING ON THE SIDE")

Note-- For whole tenderloin, do not cut pastry into rectangles. Roll to the size necessary to wrap the entire filet. Follow directions as for individual beef Wellingtons. To be used as an appetizer, wrap small pieces of tenderloin in pastry kisses and twist to close at top.

**As her husband leaves to go out of town for the week, he reminds his wife that he will be home on Friday night, which also happens to be his birthday. Once again, he reminds her that he asks for the same present every year, but never gets it.
He suggests that she practice with a ketchup bottle while he is gone. When he arrives home Friday night, he finds the front door slightly ajar. He follows a trial of rose petals to the bedroom, where his wife waits naked. Without a word, she undresses him and tells him to lie back on the bed, on his back. He can't believe he is finally going to get his birthday wish. She carefully picks up his member and encircles it lovingly with her fingers, and with the palm of her other hand, she POUNDS him!**

Tenderloin of Beef

Preheat oven 425 degrees
Serves 10 to 12

5 to 6 pounds beef tenderloin, trimmed and peeled
Fresh garlic, cut into slivers
2 large yellow onions cut into thick rounds
1 stick butter
1 Tablespoon olive oil
Paprika
Worcestershire sauce
Salt and Pepper
Marinade (see "Soak Me, Stroke Me")

To peel tenderloin, remove fat and reserve. With sharp paring knife, slide blade under membrane. Peel and discard. If you wish to marinate beef (see "NAUGHTY SAUCY"). Marinate for 1 to 3 hours.

Make 5 slits in tenderloin fat, and insert 1 garlic clove in each slit; sprinkle tenderloin with salt, pepper, and paprika.

Place roasting pan over two range burners on high heat. Add oil and butter. When very hot, add meat, onion rounds, and reserved fat. Quickly sear meat on one side. Turn meat; season. Add Worcestershire sauce and continue to sear. (Approximately 3 to 5 minutes per side).

Insert meat thermometer in thinnest part of filet. Place any remaining fat pieces and onion rounds, on top of roast and place pan in oven. Bake until desired temperature is reached, approximately, 20 to 25 minutes.

Rare-120 degrees
Medium rare-130 degrees
Well done-140 degrees

Allow to rest 15 minutes before carving. Serve with Béarnaise sauce (see "NAUGHTY SAUCY").

Excellent served with popovers and garlic fried Frenched string beans. (see "A LITTLE SOMETHING ON THE SIDE ")

A woman is having an affair when her husband comes home unexpectedly.
"Quickly" she says "take my 8 year old son and hide in the closet".
The little boy states "It's very dark in here".
"Hush" says the guy.
"Do you want to buy my baseball glove?" asks the boy.
"Hush, be quiet" the man says.
"If you don't buy it, I am going to yell"!!
"OK, how much"? "$300 "says the boy.
"That is absolutely ridiculous!" exclaims the man.
"I am going to scream and my Daddy will hear you".
"Ok, Ok" says the guy and gives the boy $ 300.
A few weeks go by and the same situation occurs.
The man rushes into the closet with the boy and the boy starts "It's dark in here"
"Hush" says the man.
"Do you want to buy my baseball?
"No" the guy whispers.
"I am going to scream" exclaims the boy!
"Ok, how much" asks the guy, disgustedly.
"$500 "says the boy.
The next day the Dad comes home and says to the son "Grab your ball and glove"!
"I can't" the son says, "I sold them".
"How much did you sell them for" the Dad inquires?
"$ 800 "admits the son.
"That is terrible" says the Dad and he drags the boy off to confession.
The little boy opens the door to the confessional, goes inside, and closes the door.
He turns to the priest and says "It's dark in here!".
"Let's not start this stuff all over again"!!! declares the priest.

hook it or cook it

Artichokes Stuffed with Shrimp

Preheat oven to 350 degrees
Raise temperature to broil
Serves 4

4 very large artichokes
Salt, lemon juice or vinegar, olive oil, pinch of baking powder
1½ pounds shrimp, raw, peeled and deveined, no tails
6 Tablespoons butter
6 scallions, chopped, including green tips
¾ teaspoon chopped garlic (or 2 garlic cloves, minced)
¾ pound mushrooms, sliced
1 cup unseasoned salad croutons
¾ teaspoon tarragon (or ¾ tablespoon fresh tarragon)
⅓ teaspoon dill (or ¾ teaspoon fresh dill)
⅓ teaspoon celery seed
⅓ teaspoon paprika
⅓ cup dry sherry
Salt and pepper, to taste
1 to 1½ cups hollandaise sauce, divided (see "NAUGHTY SAUCY")

Fill a large pasta pot, with strainer insert, with water and small amounts of salt, and vinegar or lemon juice, pinch of baking powder (to keep artichokes green) and olive oil (to keep leaves shiny), cover and bring to a rapid boil.

To prepare artichokes, cut stem short. Using scissors, trim tips of leaves, squaring them. Boil artichokes until outer leaves pull away easily and ends taste tender. Drain and cool. When artichokes are cool enough to handle, spread artichoke leaves apart and remove center, leaving a large cavity to be filled.

Filling
In a large skillet, melt butter. Add scallions, garlic and mushrooms and sauté briefly over medium heat. Add raw shrimp, tarragon, dill, celery seed, and paprika, and cook stirring constantly, until shrimp turns pink. Add sherry and croutons and simmer for 1 or 2 minutes longer. Season with salt and pepper, to taste. Remove from heat and stir in ½ cup of prepared hollandaise. Fill artichoke cavities with mixture. Spread leaves apart, stuffing mixture between the leaves. Top artichokes with remaining hollandaise. Place on foiled cookie sheet and tent with foil. Bake 10 to 15 minutes, and then remove top foil tent and place under broiler until tops are lightly browned.

Note-- cut shrimp into smaller pieces, if too large. May substitute scallops or shredded halibut, or use a seafood combination.

Barbequed Shrimp

Preheat Barbeque grill
Serves 8

2 pounds jumbo shrimp - raw, shells on (11 to 16 to the pound is best, but no smaller than 21 to 25 to the pound)
½ pound butter, melted
1 cup olive oil
8 ounces chili sauce
3 Tablespoons Worcestershire sauce
2 lemons, sliced
4 cloves garlic
3 Tablespoons lemon juice
1 Tablespoon parsley
2 teaspoons paprika
2 teaspoons oregano
2 teaspoons red pepper
1 teaspoon Tabasco
3 teaspoons liquid smoke
Salt and pepper
Grill basket

Combine all ingredients except shrimp. Cover and simmer in microwave until hot. Cool sauce before adding shrimp to marinade. Lemon juice has a tendency to toughen shrimp, so you might want to add the lemon juice fifteen minutes before grilling. Shrimp should marinate for at least three hours, but longer won't hurt

To Prepare Shrimp
Remove underneath feelers with paring knife and loosen shrimp shell with fingers - do not remove shell. Marinate shrimp in above sauce for several hours in refrigerator. Remove shrimp from sauce, reserving some sauce to serve with shrimp. Place shrimp in grill basket or on a hot grill sprayed with Pam, and grill until shrimp turn pink. Baste frequently with sauce. Turn shrimp often to prevent burning. Shrimp are cooked when they are firm and white in the center. Do not overcook shrimp, as they will toughen quickly. Shrimp left in the shell, while cooking, are more succulent but messy to eat.

Heat remaining sauce and serve over shrimp.

This recipe is delicious with **Overnight Cheese Soufflé** (see "A LITTLE SOMETHING ON THE SIDE")

Crab Defusky

Preheat oven to 350 degrees
Serves 4 people

1 pound back fin lump crab meat
½ red and ½ yellow peppers, chopped
1½ bunch scallions, chopped with tops included
Seafood Magic or crab boil seasoning, to taste
Butter
Hollandaise (see "NAUGHTY SAUCY")

Sauté vegetables in butter. Add crab and mix very lightly so as not to break up crab lumps.

Add Seafood Magic Seasoning and enough Hollandaise sauce to bind together.

Top with remaining Hollandaise sauce and bake in greased casserole or greased individual ramekins.

Bake at 350 degrees, covered, for 15 minutes, then uncovered until warm. Time is approximate depending on size of casserole and if it comes directly from the refrigerator or is at room temperature before baking. To test to see if it if hot enough, stick a metal knife all the way to the bottom of the dish and feel the blade for heat For the last minute of baking, turn bake to broil, and brown hollandaise on top. Serve over rice or pasta.

Three nuns die and arrive at the pearly gates at the exact same time. They are greeted by St. Peter himself. He tells the nuns that they must answer one question correctly in order to gain entrance to heaven. He turns to the first nun and asks her "What was the name of the first man"? "Oh that's easy, Adam" replies the nun. With that the Trumpets blow and the gates to heaven opened wide. St. Peter now turns to the second nun and asks" What was the name of the first woman"? "That was Eve" the nun correctly answers and with that the trumpets sound and the gate to heaven opened wide. "What were the first words spoken by Eve"? St. Peter asks the third nun. A puzzled look comes over the nun's face and finally she says "My, that's a hard one". And with that, the trumpets blare and the gates to heaven opened wide.

Lobster with Mushroom Buerre Blanc

3 pounds South African lobster defrosted and cut into bite size pieces.
Note-- canned lobster meat or slipper lobster can be substituted.
1 cup chopped tomatoes
10 small scallions, chopped
1 pound mushrooms, sliced without stems (save stems for sauce).
Salt & pepper

Dust lobster in flour. Sauté in butter with tomatoes and scallions. Keep warm in oven until ready to serve.

Prepare mushrooms separately. At the last minute toss sautéed lobster and mushrooms with Mushroom Buerre Blanc sauce. Serve over rice, top with mushrooms and a little salt and pepper.

Mushroom Buerre Blanc

¼ cup dry white wine
3 Tablespoons finely minced shallots
2 Tablespoons white wine vinegar
Salt & pepper
1 pound stems of fresh mushrooms
½ lb butter (2 sticks) softened, not melted
Cognac to taste

Boil white wine, shallots, vinegar, salt, pepper, and mushroom stems and reduce to 2 to 2½ tablespoons. Refrigerate. Can make early in the day.

Process 2 sticks of butter and the 2½ tablespoons of liquid. Add cognac to taste. Process until the roux is the consistency of pudding.

When lobster dish is completed, toss with sauce at the last minute and serve.

A nervous man goes to see a psychiatrist. While he is sitting in the doctor's office, he is constantly snapping his fingers. The doctor asks the man why he keeps snapping his fingers. "It's the elephants", says the patient. "What do you mean? "If I snap my fingers", says the man, "it will keep the elephants away" "The closest elephant to you is thousands of miles away" explains the doctor. "It's working" snaps the patient.

Paella

Preheat oven to 350 degrees
Serves 8 to 12 people

½ small chicken, skinned and cut into pieces
¼ pound pork, cut into small chunks
¼ pound ham, cut into small cubes
12 shrimp
½ pound flounder, cut into medium size pieces
4 clams in their shells
4 stone crab claws
4 lobster tails, shells removed, and cut into medium size pieces
18 scallops
1 medium onion, chopped
1 small green pepper, chopped
6 garlic cloves, crushed
1 small tomato, chopped
¼ teaspoon paprika
¼ teaspoon cumin
¼ teaspoon black pepper
¼ cup corn oil
½ cup white wine
1 (8-ounce) can tomato sauce
Saffron or yellow food coloring to color as desired
Salt to taste
1 pound raw rice
4 cups water or chicken broth
½ bottle of beer (optional)
Sweet green peas, chopped parsley, sliced pimento for garnish

In a large pot, place chicken pieces, pork chunks, ham, shrimp, clams, lobster, scallops, onion, green pepper, tomato, garlic and spices (reserve flounder to add later). Sprinkle oil over meats and spices; sauté over medium heat for 10 minutes. Add tomato sauce and simmer for 5 minutes. Add wine and food coloring and simmer for 5 more minutes. Add water and chicken broth and simmer for 10 to 15 minutes over low heat. Add rice and bring to a boil; boil 5 minutes.

Arrange flounder pieces over paella and place pot, covered, in 350 degree oven. Bake for 20 to 25 minutes.

Five minutes before it is done, pour ½ bottle of beer over rice (optional). Cover and return to oven for five minutes. Serve in a casserole dish and garnish with peas, parsley and pimento.

Shrimp Creole

Serves 8

4 pounds raw shrimp (15 to 25 shrimp per pound), peeled and deveined
6 Tablespoons butter, divided
4 Tablespoons olive oil
1 pound mushrooms, sliced
1/4 cup Marsala wine
2 Tablespoons each, red pepper and yellow pepper, finely minced
½ teaspoon tomato paste
2 cups ½ and ½
¼ cup sour cream
Salt, pepper, cayenne pepper, to taste
½ teaspoons dried chili pepper
2 yellow onions, sliced thin
½ teaspoon meat glaze (optional)

Heat 2 tablespoons butter and oil till foamy. Toss shrimp and cook for 1 to 2 minutes. Remove shrimp to side dish.

Add 2 tablespoons butter and sauté onions until brown and crisp. Remove and add to shrimp. Add 2 tablespoons of butter to the fry pan and add mushrooms. Cook on high heat for a few minutes, and add Marsala and peppers. Continue to cook and reduce liquid, adding more butter, if necessary. Stir in tomato paste and meat glaze (meat glaze is not readily available, but the Creole tastes great without it) Add rest of the ingredients, including shrimp and onions very slowly and simmer until sauce is heated and shrimp are pink. Adjust seasonings to taste and serve on a bed of white rice.

Jesus walks into a shop and asks the shopkeeper to make him a beautiful coat that he can wear as he speaks to people. A few days later his coat is ready.
Six months go by, and Jesus arrives back at the shopkeepers to order a new coat, only to find a very long line in front of the store. When he finally reaches the coat maker, Jesus tells him that he is very happy to see that the man has picked up a lot of clients. "I owe it all to you, because every place you go, people see your coat and want one just like it.
"We should go into business together" says Jesus. "That's a great idea" says the shop owner. "What should we call our new business?"
When they put up the new sign it read "LORD AND TAILORS"

Shrimp Scampi

Preheat oven 400 degrees
Serves 4

2 pounds jumbo shrimp (15 to 25 per pound) raw, cleaned, deveined
¼ pound butter (1 stick)
2 cloves garlic, crushed
2 Tablespoons fresh tarragon or 1 Tablespoon dried tarragon
2 teaspoons Dijon mustard
A-1 sauce, dash
Worcestershire, dash
Red wine vinegar, dash
Tabasco, dash
Lemon juice, dash
1 heaping tablespoon sour cream

Foil a large cookie sheet and evenly place shrimp, single layer.

Melt butter and add all ingredients, mixing well. Top the shrimp with ½ of the butter mixture. Turn shrimp and top shrimp with the rest of the butter mixture. Bake shrimp at 400 degrees for 8 minutes or until shrimp are firm and white in the center. Serve over a bed of white or wild and white rice.

The husband says to his wife "Honey, your birthday is coming up, why don't you go to the furrier and buy yourself a fur coat say a mink, or a chinchilla, or any fur you want"?
"I don't want a fur coat" the wife replies.
"Well then, why don't you visit the jewelry store and pick out any piece of jewelry that catches your fancy".
"I don't want jewelry" she replies.
"Ok" he goes on "how about a new car, maybe a convertible Lexus, Mercedes or even a Ferrari"
"I don't want a new car" she says.
"Well what do you want" the husband asks?
"I want a divorce" says the wife!
"I wasn't planning on spending THAT kind of money" the husbands answers.

Snapper Filet with Crabmeat Oscar

Preheat oven to 425 degrees
Serves 4

1¾ pounds snapper filets, boneless, skin removed
12 very thin asparagus spears, barely cooked
½ pound lump crabmeat (Costco Philips, Blue Star or Chicken of the Sea)
¾ cup mayonnaise
1 teaspoon dry mustard
1 teaspoon Worcestershire sauce
Juice of ½ lemon
1 Tablespoon capers, chopped
Salt and pepper, to taste
Puff pastry sheets, ⅛ inch thick, and 5x5
Egg white wash

Mix crab mixture together. Place 1 skinless filet on top of a 5x5 pastry sheet and top with 2 ounces of crab mixture and 3 partially cooked asparagus spears. Wrap fish in pastry and place seam side down on a greased baking pan. Beat egg white until foamy and brush all sides of pastry. Decorate top with extra pastry cut into shapes. Egg wash top and bake at 425 for 20 minutes or until pastry is golden in color.

Sauce
2 cups or more Hollandaise sauce (see "NAUGHTY SAUCY")
¼ cup heavy cream, whipped

Whip heavy cream and mix together with Hollandaise sauce. Top cooked pastry covered fish and serve.

An old geezer gets off his horse, ties the horse to the post, goes around to the back of the back of the horse and lifts up the horse's tail, and kisses the horse's ass. All the while, a young cowboy, standing outside the saloon, is watching. He asks the old guy why he kissed the horse's ass. "Well son", the old man said. "I have a canker sore on my lip". "I didn't know that was a cure", the surprised cowboy said. "It's not, but it sure keeps you from licking your lips!"

Grilled Salmon with Pistachio Pesto

Serves 4

4 salmon fillets, boneless, washed and patted dry
8 Tablespoons softened butter
10 large basil leaves (or ¼ cup parsley and 2 teaspoons basil)
Salt & pepper
1 clove garlic (or ½ teaspoon chopped garlic)
½ cup butter at room temperature
1 teaspoon lime juice
¼ cup lemon juice
Extra basil leaves for decoration
¼ cup shelled pistachio nuts, chopped

Place salmon in glass dish and marinate in lemon juice for ½ hour - turning once.

In food processor, place 10 basil leaves, salt and pepper, garlic, ½ cup butter, sliced, and lime juice. Process until paste forms. Add half of chopped pistachios. Sauce may be made four days ahead and stored in refrigerators. Before using, bring to room temperature so that mixture will spread easily.

Place 2 tablespoons of softened butter on non-skin side of salmon. With silver skin side up and butter side down, place salmon in a fish basket and grill fish for five minutes or until browned.

Note-- if a fish basket is not available, place salmon, butter side down, on a hot grill that has been sprayed with Pam and grill until bottom side is browned. Turn fish; placing silver skin side down. Spread top of fish with ½ of the butter paste mixture, and grill until done. Fish should look pink and moist in the middle, when split with a fork.

Remove from grill. Remove skin before placing salmon on a serving plate. Top with sauce and add rest of chopped pistachios. Decorate with extra basil leaves. (Optional)

Grilled Teriyaki Salmon with Sesame Pea Pods

Marinate fish in "Very Very Teriyaki" (purchased at local grocers) Pam hot grill grates and grill fish, as above in Grilled Salmon with Pistachio Pesto. Place poached peapods on individual dinner plates or serving platter. Arrange salmon on blanched pea pods (see "FOREPLAY") and top with toasted sesame seeds (see "HOT NUTS")

ménage à trois

Baby Rack of Lamb

Preheat oven 450 degrees
Serves 2 (4 ribs per person)

1 baby rack of lamb, 8 ribs per rack. (Suggest Costco Australian
    baby rack of lamb)
1 jar of good quality honey mustard
Salt, pepper, ad paprika
½ to 1 teaspoons thyme,
Fresh or dried rosemary

Place meat in oiled roasting pan, or four sided oven proof dish, fat side up.
Spread honey mustard on top of fat-covered meat.
Season with fresh rosemary, ½ to 1 teaspoon thyme, paprika,
Salt and pepper.

Place meat thermometer through meat of chop at narrowest end, so that it does not touch bone. Reduce oven temperature to 400 degrees. Place rack in oven and roast, uncovered, for 20 minutes and check temperature. This will give you an idea of how much longer to cook the rack, as the meat will be rarer in the center. For medium rare, thermometer should read approximately 125 to 130 degrees.

Note-- at 20 minutes, you can cut the center rib and check for doneness. If necessary, cut through the fourth rib and continue to roast in two pieces until desired doneness.

For a quicker cook, cut rack in half (4 rib section) and cook as individual portions.

Note--if lamb is too rare after cutting into chops, they can be cooked to desired pinkness by placing lettuce over and under the chops and broiling for a short time. Chops will retain their color and not turn brown or dry out.

Serve with roast garlic Bordelaise sauce or with Béarnaise sauce, (see "NAUGHTY SAUCY"). Also serve with mint jelly that may be purchased at the grocery store. (suggest Cross and Blackwell)

For large racks (not baby):
Marinate in olive oil for several hours.

Slice through thick fat, leaving just a very small amount of fat next to meat. Create a flap leaving fat still attached to meat on top of the rack. Place

continued

honey mustard and seasoning on top of meat and under flap. Cover seasonings with fat flap, but discard after roasting. Large racks may also be marinated in olive oil for several hours to tenderize.

Follow baby back directions, but increase roast time to 45 to 60 minutes. Use meat thermometer.

Suggest serving with whipped carrots, rough mashed red skinned potatoes, and thin fried onion straws (see "A Little Something on the Side")

While out of town, a golfer decides to take advantage of reciprocation at a Golf Club he is not a member of. He asks the starter if he would find someone for him to play with so that he doesn't have to play with himself.
The starter tells him to come back in thirty minutes and he'll see what he can do.
When the man returns, he finds himself paired with a newly married young couple.
She was a 42 DD. He had never seen anything like it and couldn't take his eyes off her breasts.
The husband tees off first and hooked his drive left.
The other two sliced their drive right into the woods.
As they are looking for their balls, the golfer says to the busty wife:
"I will give you $10,000 if you will let me kiss one of your boobs"
The wife is indignant but the golfer asks her to think about all the things $10,000 could buy, especially for newlyweds.
With that, the husband comes looking for the two of them.
The wife explains the proposition and the husband is furious.
Once again the golfer reminds them of what $ 10,000 could buy.
"After all it is just one kiss" he says, so the couple finally agrees and she takes off her top.
The golfer first takes one breast in his hands and then the other back and forth. The husband gets frustrated and yells, "Will you just kiss one!"
The golfer replies "If I only had the money"!!!!

Grilled Lamb Chops

Heat barbeque grill
Serves 4

1 baby rack of lamb, cut into double lamb chops, foil rib ends
    or use loin chops, cut thick
Lemon pepper

Cover ribs with foil to keep from burning. Place chops on Pam sprayed hot grill and sear one side of chops. Turn and heavily sprinkle with lemon pepper. Sear and turn to unseasoned side. Again sprinkle heavily with lemon pepper and turn and continue cooking chops until desired temperature, closing barbeque lid if necessary. Chops will feel firm to the touch when done.

Grilled Pork Chops

Heat barbeque grill
Serves 4

4 center cut loin pork chops, cut 1 ½ to 1 ¾ inches thick
Bourbon Barbeque Sauce (see "NAUGHTY SAUCY")

Baste chops with sauce and place on Pam sprayed grill. Sear for about 5 minutes and turn. Baste again with sauce. Sear and turn again. Reduce grill temperature and close cover. Turn every 5 to 8 minutes, basting each time.

Grilled Pork Tenderloin

Heat barbeque grill
Serves 6

3 pounds pork tenderloin
Pork marinade (see "SOAK ME, STROKE ME")

Marinate tenderloin overnight or for several hours. Place on Pam sprayed hot grill and sear all sides. At this point pork may be finished in a preheated oven 350 degrees or grilled till done.

Grilled Veal Chops

Heat barbeque grill
Serves 4

4 loin veal chops, 1 to 1½ inches thick
Dried Thyme, crumbled
Olive oil

Place veal chops in a baggie and sprinkle generously with crumbled thyme. Cover with olive oil and marinate for 1 hour. Remove chops from baggie and place on very hot Pam sprayed grill and cook 5 minutes on each side. Top with **Butter D'Hotel** (see "NAUGHTY SAUCY"), season with salt and pepper and serve. Accompany with baked sweet potatoes.

General Custer is making his last stand. He goes to the sentry and asks: "Have you seen any Indians far away beyond the mountains?"
"No" says the Look out.
"Keep watching" says Custer "I'll check back every hour."
When he returns again, he asks the same question of the soldier.
"Have you seen any Indians"?
"Yes"
"How tall is he" asks Custer?
Putting his thumb and forefinger about two inches apart, he indicates that the Indian he sees is very small and therefore must be far away.
Each hour, General Custer checks with the sentry and asks "How tall is the Indian"?
Each time the sentry increases the space between his thumb and forefinger, indicating that the Indian is getting bigger each hour and therefore must be getting a lot closer.
"How big is he now?" questions Custer.
"Oh, he is very big now" says the Look out.
"Shoot him" yells Custer!
"I can't" says the Look out.
"Why not?" screams Custer.
Putting his thumb and forefinger close together, the Sentry says: "Because I have known him since he was THIS BIG "!!!!

Pork Chops with Roasted Garlic Cranberry Bordelaise

Preheat oven to 350 degrees
Serves 2

Olive oil
1 Tablespoon roasted garlic cloves, diced (can be purchased)
2 Tablespoons shallots, diced
½ Tablespoon celery, diced fine
½ Tablespoon raw carrot, diced fine
⅓ cup amber-color sherry (not cream sherry)
2-3 Tablespoons dry cranberries
2 center cut loin pork chops, 1½" thick, washed and patted dry
½ cup veal demi glaze, available at food specialty stores (or beef or chicken consumé)
1 Tablespoon butter
Fresh sage, very small amount, leaves cut into small pieces

To roast garlic
Preheat oven to 350 degrees. Put small amount of olive oil in very small oven-proof container (a measuring cup works well). Add garlic cloves in their own skin, or a whole garlic bulb with top cut off and cloves spread apart. Bake until garlic is soft. Elephant garlic bulbs work best.

Bordelaise Sauce
Add small amount of olive oil to heavy sauté pan and cook celery, shallots, and carrot. Add garlic and sauté until soft. Do not burn garlic. Deglaze pan with 1/3 cup sherry. Reduce to syrup. Add demi glaze and reduce by ¼. Add cranberries.

Note-- Bordelaise may be made well ahead. Just before serving, add one tablespoon butter and sage.

To Grill Pork Chops
Have grill or heavy skillet very hot and brown chops on both sides. If grilling, use Bordelaise sauce to baste. Salt and pepper chops after searing. Chops can now be finished off by baking in 350 degree oven until slightly pink and juicy.

To finish chops by grilling, turn grill flame to low. Continue basting with sauce, turning every 5 minutes. Close grill lid. Depending on thickness of chop and grill, chops will take about 25 minutes. If you cut into them, chops should be lightly pink and juicy.

Veal Chops with Mushrooms

Serves 4

4 veal loin chops, 1¼" thick
8 Tablespoons butter, divided
¼ cup flour
1 teaspoon salt
⅛ teaspoon pepper
2 cups sliced onion
½ clove garlic, crushed
1 cup veal demi glaze, available at food specialty stores (or beef or chicken consommé)
½ pound sliced mushrooms
2 teaspoons lemon juice
1 teaspoon fresh tarragon
½ teaspoon fresh chives
1 teaspoon liquid gravy seasoning
¾ cup dry white wine

Trim excess fat from chops; rinse and pat dry. Roll up end (tail) and secure with a toothpick. Melt 3 tablespoons butter in an electric fry pan. Add chops and brown on both sides. Remove chops and place on to platter. Add onions and garlic to fry pan, and sauté, adding more butter, as needed, to keep onions from burning. Remove onions and garlic, and set aside, while you make the gravy.

In separate pan, sauté mushrooms in 1 tablespoon of butter and set aside.

Gravy
Melt 4 tablespoons of butter in the electric fry pan. Add flour and cook for a few minutes, to burn off the flour taste. Add demi glaze or consommé and wine to flour, a little at a time, smoothing out any lumps. Add seasoning and Gravy Master (or gravy booster). Return chops to pan. Add sautéed mushrooms, onions, and garlic. Cover and simmer for about 30 minutes, or until chops are tender.

Serve chops, spooning gravy on top of chops.

Veal Scaloppini Marsala

Serves 2-4

1 pound veal scallops, pounded thin
Flour, seasoned with salt, pepper, and paprika
⅛ pound very thin prosciutto ham
½ pound mushrooms, sliced and sautéed in separate pan
3 Tablespoons butter
1 Tablespoon olive oil
¼ cup Marsala wine
2 Tablespoons veal demi glaze or 2 Tablespoons beef consommé
1 teaspoon parsley, chopped
1 teaspoon lemon juice

Place veal between two sheets of parchment paper, or plastic wrap, and pound to ⅛ thick. Cut into medallions

Place seasoned flour in a baggie. Dip medallions into the flour and shake off excess flour

Add butter and oil to a large skillet or electric fry pan and heat.
Add veal pieces, a few at a time, and sauté until veal is browned on both sides. Remove to side platter. Add ham and sauté, and then set aside.

To make gravy, avert eyes (turn head away for a moment) and add ¼ cup Marsala to meat pan and cook for 1 minute. Add 2 tablespoons demi glaze OR 2 tablespoons beef consommé and stir until smooth, making sure that you have scraped in all of the pan drippings

Stir in 1 teaspoon parsley and 1 teaspoon lemon juice. Taste gravy and make any adjustments to seasonings, as necessary.

Return meat, ham and mushrooms to pan. Toss with gravy until all pieces are coated. Simmer until veal is tender and serve.

A man asks a pharmacist "If I take Viagra, can I get it over the counter?"

The Pharmacist replies "only if it's a narrow counter"!!!!!!!!!

Veal Foyot

Preheat oven 200-225 degrees

2 pounds boneless, loin of veal, cut into 4 equal cutlets
½ teaspoon salt
¼ teaspoon pepper
1 Tablespoon butter
¼ cup finely chopped onions
¼ cup bread crumbs
¼ cup grated Swiss cheese
½ cup dry white wine
3 Tablespoons butter, melted

Place veal cutlets in a greased shallow baking dish, and season with salt and pepper.

Heat 1 tablespoon of butter, in small skillet. Add onions and cook until golden.

In a bowl, combine bread crumbs and Swiss cheese. Spread 1 tablespoon of cooked onions on each cutlet. Cover with crumb mixture. Press cutlets with flat edge of knife, or palm of your hand, to make mixture stick. Sprinkle remaining onions around in dish. Pour wine around meat in the dish. Drizzle melted butter over cutlets. Bake in preheated oven at 200 to 250 degrees, uncovered, for 2 hours.

The kindergarten is practicing for the Christmas play. One little boy complains to his parents that he has been cast as in Innkeeper who turn Joseph, Mary and the baby Jesus away, when they knock at the door of the Inn and ask for a place to sleep. They explain to the little boy, that this is a play and he has to repeat the words that are in the script, even if that isn't really how he felt. So on the night of the play, Joseph, Mary and baby Jesus arrives at the Innkeepers door. They are met by the little boy, playing the part of the Innkeeper.
He says" I'm very sorry. There is no room at the inn, but won't you come in for cocktails?"

Barbecued Lemon Duckling

Preheat grill

4 ½ - 5 pound duckling, quartered
¼ cup lemon juice
¼ cup butter, melted
½ teaspoon freshly ground black pepper
1 Tablespoon salt
2 Tablespoons paprika
1 Tablespoon brown sugar
Pam

Mix ingredients together. Pour over duck, then cover and chill 2 to 4 hours.

In the center, place a drip pan large enough to cover the area under the ducks. With grill top up, avert eyes, and carefully spray grates with Pam.

Cook duck quarter about 45 minutes, remove drip pan and continue to cook duck until skin is crisp and duck is fully cooked. Continue basting duck the entire time it is cooking.

Serve with orange sauce.

A man and his new retriever, go duck hunting. When a bevy of ducks flew overhead, the hunter took aim and shot a duck, which fell to the water. "Go fetch the duck" the man said to the dog. The dog got out of the boat, walked across the water, retrieved the duck, and walked back to the boat and got on board. The man could not believe what he had just seen.
When the next group of ducks flew by, the hunter once again shot a duck. Once again, he told the dog to get the duck. The dog repeated the same process. The man thought "No one is going to believe this", so when he went home, he called his brother and invited him to go duck hunting with him the following Saturday.
The hunter, his brother and the retriever are in the boat. When the first duck is shot, the man turns to his brother and says "You won't believe what you are about to see" and he tells the dog to fetch the duck. The dog gets out of the boat, walks across the water, picks up the duck in his mouth, and walks back across the water and gets into the boat. The man says to his brother "Can you believe THAT"? "No "says the brother. "I've never seen a retriever that couldn't swim".

lotsapastabilities

Pasta Alfredo

Serves 6

⅔ cups heavy cream
½ cup butter (1 stick)
1½ cups grated fresh Parmesan cheese, divided
¼ teaspoon salt
Pinch of pepper
12 ounces pasta cooked and drained

Optional
Chopped parsley, sautéed mushrooms, sautéed, colored peppers, julienne, baby peas, steamed broccoli pieces

Heat butter and cream in a sauce pan, until all the butter is melted. Add 1 cup Parmesan cheese, salt and pepper. Stir until everything is well blended, and the sauce is smooth. Toss over drained noodles. And sprinkle with remaining cheese. Top with any of the optional items. Serve immediately.

Bucatini

Serves 4

1 pound pasta
½ cup olive oil
½ pound bacon
Pepper
¼ pound prosciutto
2 egg yolks
¼ cup baby peas, cooked
¼ cup sliced mushrooms, sautéed
6 ounces grated Parmesan and Romano cheese mixed

Cook pasta in rapidly boiling salted water until tender. Drain.
Sauté bacon in olive oil until crisp. Add 4 pinches of black pepper and allow to stand for a minute. Add prosciutto and stir over heat for 1 minute. Stir in peas and mushrooms and continue to cook for 2 minutes.

Toss cooled pasta with slightly beaten eggs yolks (if pasta is too hot, it will cook the egg). Add bacon mixture, including any bacon fat and oil in the pan. Toss gently and add in cheeses and toss again. Serve.

Note-- this dish is excellent when served with angel hair pasta. Add fresh basil leaves and toss on toasted pine nuts. (see "HOT NUTS")

Easy Penne Pasta with Tomato Cream Vodka Sauce

Serves 4

2 cans recipe ready diced tomatoes with seasonings (28 ounces total)
1 small onion, chopped
1 teaspoon jarred chopped garlic
1 cup heavy cream
¼ cup vodka
¼ teaspoon dried crushed red pepper flakes
1 Tablespoon butter
1 Tablespoon olive oil
1 pound penne pasta
Fresh grated fresh imported Parmesan
Fresh chives, finely chopped

Sauté onion and garlic in oil until the onions are translucent.
Drain diced tomatoes and puree in food processor. Pour pureed tomatoes into large sauce pan and add onion, garlic, red pepper flakes, and cream. Heat until cream has thickened the sauce, adding more cream if necessary. Heat butter in small pan and add vodka. Blend and add to tomato sauce. Sauce can be made well ahead and refrigerated or frozen.

Cook pasta in a large amount of boiling, salted water. Add some olive oil to the water to keep pasta from sticking. Stir occasionally. Cook until noodles are tender. Drain.

Bring sauce to simmer and toss with pasta. Top with fresh grated Parmesan and chives.

A lady inserted an ad in the classifieds:
"Husband Wanted"
The next day she received 100 replies.
They all said the same thing:
"You can have mine!"

Linguini with Clams and Shrimp

Serves 4

¼ pound butter (1 stick), melted
2 Tablespoons garlic, minced
3 Tablespoons chopped fresh parsley
2 seven ounce cans, minced clams
1 bottle clam juice
¼ cups white wine, optional
1 pound raw shrimp, shelled and deveined
1 pound linguini
1 Tablespoon olive oil
Salt, to taste

Fill a large pasta pot with water and bring to a rapid boil. Add salt, olive oil, and partially cook pasta, until the noodles are al dente. Noodles will continue cooking in the clam mixture. When noodles are almost done, remove from heat and drain. Rinse noodles with cold water.

Combine wine, clam juice, minced clams, minced garlic, and melted butter. Add partially cooked pasta, and raw shrimp. When the shrimp turn pink (white inside) and the linguini is desired consistency, the dish is ready to serve.

A young couple is having trouble conceiving and go to a fertility doctor for help. He takes the necessary tests and tells the couple that there is no medical reason to keep them from conceiving. He suggests that they relax and have sex whenever the spirit moves them, instead of the regimented sex life they had described to him. One year later, the doctor bumps into the couple and is delighted to see them pushing a baby carriage. Thrilled, he says to them "I guess my suggestion worked!" "Yes" said the husband, "But they'll never let us in Wal Mart again!"

a little something on the side

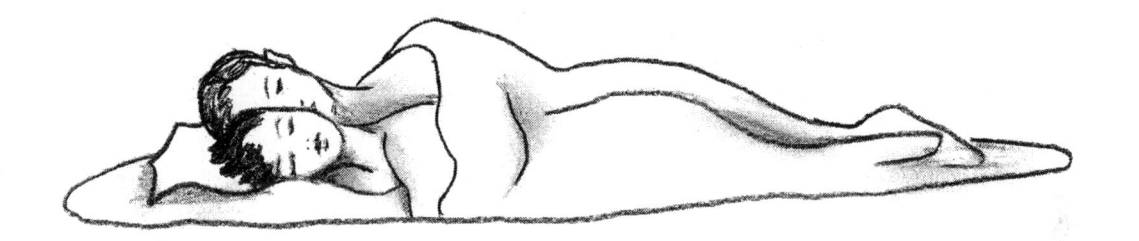

Apple Stuffing

¼ cup butter
1 green apple, peeled and sliced
1 medium onion
3 slices white bread
3 slices whole wheat bread
½ teaspoon brown sugar
1 teaspoon salt
½ teaspoon pepper
½ teaspoon poultry seasoning

Melt butter. Sauté apples and onions until lightly browned. Break bread into pieces and moisten with water. Add brown sugar and seasonings to bread. Add bread to apples; sauté until brown. Add more butter if needed. Mix lightly, taste, and add more seasoning if needed.

Use with Cornish game hens or as an alternate stuffing in turkey.

Apples with Jack

Use ¼ to ½ apples per person

Assorted apples, Granny Smith, Red Delicious, Fuji, Macintosh, skin on, cored and sliced in food processor or by hand
Butter
Apple Butter
Jack Daniels or Wild Turkey

In a heavy fry pan, melt butter and apple butter. Add sliced apples, reserving some of the Granny Smith for later. Sauté apples until they soften, adding more apple butter as needed to prevent sticking. Add the rest of the apples and the Jack Daniels to taste.

Can be stored in refrigerator or frozen. Heat and serve. Apples are excellent with pork, lamb or chicken.

Bumper sticker seen in Alaska
Definition of vegetarian---
Old Indian name for "BAD HUNTER"

Cheesy Crusted Cauliflower

Preheat oven 350 degrees
Serves 6

1 large head cauliflower
½ cup mayonnaise
2½ Tablespoons Dijon mustard
1 cup or more grated sharp Cheddar cheese

Remove stalk and outer leaves. Using vegetable peeler, remove any spots leaving cauliflower head whole. Wash. Steam cauliflower over boiling salted water, until tender (about 15 to 20 minutes) drain well. This can be done well ahead of time. Place head in a microwavable dish. Combine mayonnaise and mustard and spread evenly over cauliflower. Cover with cheddar cheese, wrap loosely with plastic wrap or cover with parchment paper and microwave on high for 20 seconds or until cheese is melted or bake in preheated oven 350 degrees for 10 minutes or until cheese is melted. Serve as whole cauliflower.

Tomato, Broccoli Cauliflower Baskets

Serves 8

8 large tomatoes
1 small head cauliflower
Broccoli florets
Hollandaise (see "NAUGHTY SAUCY")

With a sharp knife, and starting ½ half inch from center of tomato top, cut half way down, removing tomato top, but leaving about a 1" handle intact. Remove insides of tomato and set aside while you prepare the other tomato baskets.

In steamer basket, place cauliflower and cook over salted boiling water until tender or microwave. Cool and cut into florets.

Place broccoli florets in a steamer basket, adding a pinch of baking powder to the boiling water. When tender, run under cold water to stop the cooking and refrigerate.

To assemble
Fill tomatoes with broccoli and cauliflower, carefully place tomatoes in a greased baking dish. Bake at 350 degrees until warm. Top with warm hollandaise and serve.

Cheesy Potatoes

Preheat oven 350 degrees
Serves 10 to 12

1 32 ounce bag of frozen hash brown potatoes
2 cups sharp cheddar cheese, grated
1 can cream of chicken soup
2 cups (1 pint) sour cream
½ cup yellow onion, chopped
½ cup butter, melted
1 teaspoon salt
½ teaspoon pepper
2½ cups corn flakes, crushed
¼ cup butter, melted

In a large bowl, mix frozen potatoes, cheese, soup, sour cream, onion, salt, and ½ cup melted butter. Place in a greased 9x12 baking pan. At this point, potatoes may be wrapped and frozen. It is not necessary to defrost before baking, but the baking time will be longer

When ready to bake, place corn flakes in a sealable baggie and crush with your hands. Add in ¼ cup melted butter and spread mixture on top of potatoe mixture. Bake mixture uncovered, for 1 hour in 350 degree oven or until potatoes are hot. Make sure the corn flakes brown but do not burn. To test doneness, stick the point of a metal knife through to the bottom of the pan. Withdraw the knife and feel if the tip is warm. (If potatoes are frozen, bake for ½ hour without corn flakes. Remove from oven and top with buttered corn flakes and continue to bake until hot.)

Note-- to use as main course, add ham, pork, beef, chicken or seafood to the potato mixture.

A woman wakes up very early and realizes her husband is not in bed. She goes down stairs and finds her husband sitting in a chair in the kitchen - facing the window. He is watching the sun come up and tears are falling from his eyes.
"What's the matter honey"? She asks
"Do you remember 25 years ago when your father found us making love and told me either to marry you or go to jail?" he replies
"Well I would have gotten out today!!"

Chili Rellano

Preheat oven 350 degrees

2 small cans whole green chilies
4 eggs
2 cups milk
⅓ cup flour
Salt and pepper
Monterey jack cheese or Mexican blend, grated
½ pound mild cheddar cheese, grated

Open can of chilies and drain. Split open, but leave whole. Wipe out seeds. Stuff with Monterey Jack cheese. Place seam side down in greased baking pan, single layer. Mix eggs, milk, salt and pepper, and flour. Pour over chilies and top with cheddar cheese. Bake 350 degrees for 45 minutes. Serve immediately.

Mom and Dad are entertaining company when their six year old little girl comes in to say goodnight.
One her way out of the room, the little girl asks her Mommy "Where do babies come from"?
The Mom, not wanting to get into a long discussion says "The Daddy plants a seed in Mommy's tummy and that's where the babies come from"
This explanation seems to satisfy the little girl. But as she leaves the room, she turns to her Mom and once again asks "Does the Mommy swallow the seed"?
"No dear" says the Mom" that is where jewelry comes from!!!"

Coconut Sweet Potato Casserole

Preheat oven 350 degrees
Serves 8

3 cups mashed sweet potatoes or yams (canned or fresh cooked)
1 cup sugar
½ teaspoon salt
5⅓ Tablespoons butter (1/3 stick)
½ cup milk or cream
1 teaspoon vanilla
½ teaspoon coconut flavoring

Mix the above ingredients and put in greased baking dish. Spread topping and bake 350 for 35 minutes

Topping
1 cup brown sugar
⅓ cup flour
5⅓ Tablespoons butter (1/3 stick)
½ cup chopped pecans
½ cup coconut

Mix together and spread on top of sweet potato casserole.

Marshmallow Sweet Potatoes

Preheat oven 350 degrees, then preheat broiler
Serves 8

6 sweet potatoes or yams, boiled till tender, cooled and peeled
½ pound butter (2 sticks or more), cut into chunks
Light brown sugar
Maple syrup
1 large bag of large sized marshmallows

In a large casserole, slice cooked potatoes the long way, into quarters. Layer potatoes, brown sugar, butter chunks, and pour maple syrup over layer. Repeat layering, until all the potatoes have been used. (The amount of sugar, syrup, and butter is unimportant, as you can never use too much) Bake casserole, uncovered, for about 45 minutes to 1 hour, basting potatoes with juices every 15 minutes. Remove from oven. Raise oven temperature to broil. Just before serving, top with marshmallows and run under broiler till marshmallows are lightly browned. Do not allow to burn, so watch carefully. Remove from oven and serve.

Corn Casserole

Preheat oven 350 degrees

1 can corn niblets, do not drain juice
1 can cream corn
1 package Martha White "sweet" cornbread mix (available at Wal-Mart)
¼ pound (1 stick) butter

Melt butter and combine all ingredients in a bowl. Lightly spray Pam on a 10x8 casserole dish. Pour ingredients into the casserole and bake, uncovered, at 350 degrees, for about 45 minutes or until golden brown.

Fiesta Corn

Canned corn or cooked corn cut off kernel
Fresh Tomatoes, chopped
Sweet onion, chopped finely
Red, yellow, and orange pepper, chopped
Salt and pepper

Heat corn, add other ingredients and heat slightly and serve.

Three friends declare undying friendship and agree to carry out each other's wishes.
So when Paddy dies, his two best friends put his body in a row boat so that he can have the burial at sea which he requested.
So out the row:
"Do you think we are deep enough?"
"I am not sure" says Shawn" but I will jump in and see."
The water is only to his knees, so they keep on rowing.
"Are we deep enough yet" asks Shawn again.
"I don't know, but I'll jump in and find out". The water is only to his waist, so they keep on rowing
They continue to row, but they are getting very tired and realize that they have to row back home.
"What about now"? Shawn jumps into the water, but alas, it is only to his chest, so they row further. Finally they try again. Shawn jumps in the water, but does not come up. Eventually he surfaces and declares "it is finally deep enough".
"You can give me the shovel NOW" says Shawn.

Fried Rice with Barbequed Pork

Serves 8 to 10

4 cups cooked rice (day old)
3 eggs, beaten
4 scallions (green onions) chopped including tops
4 large dried shitake mushrooms, prepared and chopped, and baby peas, or your choice of vegetables
1 teaspoon salt
½ cup of Chinese barbequed pork (or any left over meat, chicken, ham, pork, seafood, or beef)
2 Tablespoons mushroom soy sauce (or all purpose soy)
½ teaspoon MSG (optional)
8 Tablespoons oil, divided

To make egg pancakes:
In a heavy fry pan, heat a little oil. When hot, add a thin layer of beaten egg. When lightly browned on bottom, flip and brown on other side. Remove from pan and set aside, while you continue to make egg pancakes, until all the egg is used up. Cut pancakes into bite sized pieces.

Barbequed Pork

Preheat oven 350 degrees

3 pounds pork tenderloin or pork butt
½ teaspoon salt
¼ teaspoon pepper
¼ teaspoon Chinese 5 spices
1 teaspoon dry sherry
2 Tablespoons soy sauce
3 Tablespoons hoisin sauce
½ teaspoons red food coloring

Marinate pork in salt, pepper, 5 spices, sherry, soy sauce, food coloring, hoisin sauce, and marinate for least 2 to 48 hours. Place pork on top of broiler pan that has slats to allow marinade to drip through while baking. Bake at 350 degrees for about 25 minutes, turning pork so that all sides get roasted. Pork is done when inside is light pink and juicy. Remove from oven and cool. When cool, slice diagonally. (See "Foreplay" to serve as hors d'oeuvre)

To prepare mushrooms
Soak dried mushrooms in boiling water to cover, for 20 minutes or until soft.

continued

To fry rice
In wok with collar, heat 2 tablespoons sesame oil. Add onions, mushrooms, and desired vegetables and stir fry until tender. Remove vegetables and set aside.

Brown cooked rice in 4 tablespoons of sesame oil. Add soy sauce, MSG (optional) and stir fry. Add cooked vegetables, barbequed pork, peas, and egg pancakes. Adjust all seasonings and serve.

Note-- as an alternative to barbequed pork, grill center cut pork chops, basted in Jack Daniels Barbeque Sauce (see "NAUGHTY SAUCY" and "A FARE TO REMEMBER" Grilled Pork Chops)

Garlic Broccoli Florets with Cashews

Serves 6

2 heads of broccoli
1 Tablespoon brown sugar
3 Tablespoons soy sauce
2 teaspoons white vinegar
⅓ cup butter
1 teaspoon chopped garlic, in a jar
¼ teaspoon pepper
⅓ cup cashews

Wash broccoli and cut off stems, placing them in the bottom of a deep steamer basket or pasta pot. Place tops of broccoli on top of stems. Place basket over boiling, salted water. Add a pinch of baking soda to keep the broccoli a bright green. Cover and steam about six minutes or until tender. Arrange on serving platter or individual plates. Melt butter in microwave and stir in brown sugar, soy sauce, vinegar, pepper, and garlic. Microwave on high for 45 seconds or until mixture boils. Stir in cashews. Pour over broccoli and serve immediately.

Sesame Asparagus

1 bunch asparagus, very thin, or peeled
Sesame seeds
Sesame oil
Wok with collar
Break asparagus and discard tough ends. Heat oil in wok and add asparagus, sprinkle with sesame seed, stir fry and serve.

Beer Fritter Cover Batter

2 eggs
½ cup milk
1 cup corn flakes, crushed
1 cup flour, plus extra baggie of flour for dipping
2 Tablespoons dry mustard
¼ teaspoon salt
¼ teaspoon pepper
2 Tablespoons baking powder
½ cup beer (more if necessary)
Frying oil (preferably peanut oil)

Combine all dry ingredients in a bowl. Make a well. Beat eggs and milk together and pour into well. Add beer and mix. Cover and let stand at least three hours. Batter should be consistency of whipping cream. Add more beer if batter gets too thick. Fill an electric fryer with peanut oil and heat to 375 degrees. Dip items to be fried, first into flour, shaking off excess flour, and then dip pieces into batter and fry until golden brown. If necessary, sprinkle with paprika, before frying. This will quicken the browning process.

Suggested Fritters raw vegetables, seafood, fruit, cheese. To fry cheese, first freeze the cheese pieces before battering and frying. To fry shell fish, add a little oil to your batter. When making fruit fritters, add a little sugar to your batter.

Beer Batter

1 cup flour
⅛ teaspoon baking soda
2 teaspoons salt
¾ teaspoon pepper
Paprika (optional for browning)
1 egg
1 cup beer (no foam)
Extra flour for dredging

Mix dry ingredients and place in a bowl. Make a well in the flour mixture. Beat egg with a fork and mix into beer. Pour wet mixture into flour well and stir until smooth. Cover and allow to sit for three hours. Heat oil in electric fryer to 375 degrees and dredge items to be fried first in flour shaking off excess flour before dipping in beer batter. Place items in fry basket, and fry until golden brown. If necessary, sprinkle items with paprika, to speed up the browning process. This may be important, as you do not want to overcook small items.

Make Day Ahead Cheese Soufflé

Preheat oven 350 degrees
Serve 6 to 8
Total baking time 1½ hours

8 slices day old white bread, crusts removed
10 ounces sharp cheddar cheese grated
5 eggs, beaten
2 cups milk
Salt, pepper, and a dash of cayenne pepper
¼ cup butter, melted

Twenty-four hours ahead, crumble bread into a greased small soufflé dish or casserole. Add cheese and toss with bread. Beat eggs milk, and seasonings. Pour over bread and refrigerate for 24 hours.

Day of serving, top with ¼ cup melted butter and bake at 350 degrees covered for ½ hour. Uncover and continue baking for an additional hour. Serve immediately as soufflé will fall.

Note-- for large soufflé dish, make recipe 1 ½ times.

A man sees an ad in the newspaper for a talking dog. He calls the number in the ad and asks if he can come over and se the dog. When he gets to the seller's house, he asks to see the dog. The dog actually is beautiful and very friendly.
"Does your dog really talk?", the prospective buyer inquires.
"Yes" says the dogs owner. "Ask him whatever you would like"
So the man says to the dog "So, what have you been doing lately?"
The dog says, "Well for the last four years, I've been adviser to President Bush. Before that, I advised President Clinton, and I have also helped out at the FED."
The dog buyer cannot believe what he has just witnessed and he says to the owner "Why are you selling this amazing dog?"
"Lies, all lies" says the owner.

Rough Mashed Red Skin Potatoes

3 pounds small red skin #B creamers, scrubbed clean, skins on
Milk
½ pound of butter, or to taste
Salt and pepper, to taste

Fill a very large pot with water, cover and bring to a rapid boil. Add potatoes and boil about 40 minutes, or until sharp knife slides cleanly through the potato. Drain. Using a hand potato masher, or electric beaters, whip the potatoes until they are almost smooth (There will still be some lumps) Add milk, salt, pepper, and plenty of butter, and beat until blended. If not using immediately, potatoes may be placed in a freezer baggie and frozen or refrigerated before using. Open baggie slightly, before heating, and micro wave on high. Whip potatoes before serving, adding more milk and butter if necessary.

Roasted Red Skins

Preheat oven to 400 degrees

3 pounds red skin #B potatoes, washed and cleaned, skins on
¼ pound butter, or more if needed
Salt and pepper

Place potatoes in baking pan. Season with salt and pepper, top with pats of butter and bake at 400 degrees for 40 minutes or until potatoes are tender. Cut potatoes into quarters, and roll around in the browned butter, or spoon the butter on top of the potatoes before serving.

Garlic Roasted Potatoes

1 ½ pounds red skin #B potatoes
Garlic, minced
Asiago cheese
Butter, melted

Bake potatoes, following directions for Roasted Red Skins, or microwave potatoes until the insides are soft. Using a melon scoop, spoon or sharp knife, remove most of the potato, being careful to leave a border of potato next to the shin. Fill cavity with cheese, minced garlic and brush the top with butter. Bake or broil in oven, until of potato is hot and top has browned.

Southern Sweet Potato Pie

Preheat oven to 375 degrees
Serves 6 to 8

Crust
1 pre made 9" pastry shell, partially baked

Filling
1 to ½ cups, cooked, skinned, and mashed sweet potato (or canned)
¼ cup butter, softened
¾ cup light brown sugar
¼ teaspoon nutmeg
¼ teaspoon ground cloves
¼ teaspoon salt
½ teaspoon cinnamon
3 eggs, separated, room temperature
½ cup heavy cream
¼ cup milk
¼ cup either Bourbon or Dark Rum (my preference)

In a small bowl, beat egg yolks until thick and lemon yellow.
In food processor, combine butter, sugar and mashed sweet potato. Add egg beaten yolks, cream and milk, cinnamon, salt, nutmeg, cloves, and Bourbon or rum and process until smooth, creating sweet potato custard. Remove to large bowl.

In a separate bowl, beat room temperature egg whites until stiff, but not dry (peaks will appear when beaters are lifted from the egg whites)

Fold in ¼ of beaten egg whites to potato custard and stir till blended. Gently fold in remaining egg whites to potato custard, when blended, pour into partially baked pie crust.

Topping
¼ cup butter, softened
¼ cup flour
¼ cup light brown sugar
¼ cup pecans, chopped

In food processor, combine butter, flour, and sugar. Remove to bowl and stir in nuts. Sprinkle topping over pie and bake in the middle oven rack at 375 for 40 minutes, or until golden brown.

Spinach Noodle Ring

Preheat oven 350 degrees
Serves 12

12 ounces broad egg noodles
4 - 10 ounce packages of frozen chopped spinach
1 large yellow onion, chopped
½ cup butter
5 eggs, slightly beaten
½ cup sour cream
1 pound fresh mushrooms, sliced
1 Tablespoon butter
½ teaspoon salt
Oil

Cook noodles in a large pot of boiling water, to which you have added salt and oil. Drain noodles, when noodles are barely tender, (al dente).

Defrost spinach in microwave and drain well by squeezing the spinach between sheets of paper towel to extract all the water. Combine noodles and spinach and set aside. Sauté onions in melted butter until lightly browned. Add to noodle mixture. Stir in beaten eggs, sour cream, and salt, and blend well. Pour into a 1 ½ quart well greased ring mold. Place mold in a pan of hot water and bake at 350 degrees for 45 minutes.

15 minutes before serving, sauté mushrooms in 2 tablespoon butter.

To remove from mold
Run a sharp knife around the edges of the mold and place the mold quickly in a hot water bath. Remove immediately and place a serving platter over top of mold and invert. Remove mold and fill center of ring with cooked mushrooms.

Mr. and Mrs. Wong are anxiously awaiting the arrival of their first born. When the Doctor presents them with a baby of a different color, they are shocked. They ask the doctor how this could be and the doctor explains " Two Wongs do not make a white!"

Spinach with White Raisins

Serves 5 people

2 pounds fresh baby spinach, cooked and drained
⅓ cup white raisins soaked in white wine till plump, then drained
¼ cup olive oil
¼ cup pine nuts
2 tablespoons finely chopped fresh parsley
Salt and pepper

Heat oil and sauté pine nuts briefly until lightly browned. Stir in the spinach and the raisins. Add salt and pepper to taste and sauté over low heat for about 5 minutes. Serve immediately.

Serve with salmon or lamb.

Easy Creamed Spinach

Serves 2

1 ½ pounds of fresh baby spinach or chopped frozen spinach
    microwave and squeezed very dry in paper towels
3 ounces cream cheese
Salt and pepper
Grated onion

In a large pot, rapidly boil water, adding salt and a pinch of baking soda. Dip spinach quickly into boiling water and blanch quickly. Drain and place between paper towels and squeeze very dry. Place all Ingredients in a blender or food processor and puree. This can be done way ahead of time. When ready to serve, heat in microwave and serve immediately.

Mr. and Mrs. Jones, go to play golf. The husband tees off first from the black tips. All of a sudden there is a blood curdling scream comes from the red tees. He rushes to his wife, only to find her dead. The police arrive to find a distraught husband. It is easy to see that there has been a terrible accident. The husband did not do this on purpose. However, the next morning the police call. "I thought we cleared all this up yesterday. "Well, said the policeman, the autopsy showed a second ball up your wife's butt"
"Oh" explains the husband that was my mulligan"!

Sweet Potato Pancakes with Citrus and Cranberry Relish

Preheat oven 350 degrees

6 eggs, lightly beaten
1 cup whole wheat flour
1 teaspoon baking powder
1 teaspoon salt
⅛ teaspoon cayenne pepper
1 medium sweet potato raw, peeled and grated
½ cup sharp cheddar cheese, grated
1 teaspoon fresh or dried thyme (extra for garnish)
1 large egg lightly beaten
1½ cup milk
½ cup vegetable oil for frying

Sauce

1 medium unpeeled orange, scrubbed, halved, seeded, and cut into 2 inch chunks
1 medium Granny Smith apple, peeled cored, and cut into 2 inch chunks
¼ unpeeled medium lemon, seeded and chunked
2 cups fresh or frozen cranberries (not canned)
½ cup sugar
½ cup walnuts, chopped

To make sauce

Add orange, apple, and lemon to food processor and finely chop. Add cranberries and coarsely chop. You want cranberries to be chunky. Transfer to a bowl. Stir in sugar and walnuts. You may refrigerate the sauce, for one week.

To assemble pancakes

In a small bowl, sift together the flour, baking powder, salt, and pepper. Add sweet potato, cheese, and thyme. In medium bowl, combine 6 beaten eggs and milk. Add dry ingredients Stir, just until mixed. Heat 1 tablespoon of oil in a large skillet. Drop pancake batter, about 3 inches in diameter, onto well greased skillet. When browned, turn and brown other side of pancake. Top each pancake with 1 tablespoon of sauce, and serve.

To make pancakes ahead

Pancakes may be cooked 1 day ahead. Place cooked pancakes between sheets of parchment paper, then wrap in plastic wrap, and foil. Refrigerate or freeze. To reheat, drop into hot fat and quickly crisp pancake, or layer cooked pancakes, single layer, on a cookie sheet, and bake at 350 degrees until warm.

Combination Pancakes

Preheat fat to 375 degrees

1 cup raw white potatoes, soaked in cold water for several hours, drained and grated (or frozen shoe string potatoes)
1 cup raw sweet potato, soaked in cold water for several hours, drained and grated
2 whole eggs
Pinch of baking powder
1½ teaspoon salt and a pinch of pepper
1 Tablespoon flour
Oil for frying
Apple sauce
Sour cream

Beat eggs and add to grated potatoes with the rest of the ingredients. Heat a large spider or heavy fry pan, add oil and drop potato mixture by spoonfuls, leaving plenty of space between the cakes. For very crisp pancakes, fry in 1/8 inches of oil, or drop pancakes on a well greased hot spider. Turn pancakes to brown and remove from pan and drain on paper towel.

To serve as an appetizer-- top warm pancake with sour cream and applesauce.

Heavenly Potato Pancakes

2 cups raw, grated shoe string potatoes (or 4 raw white potatoes, soaked for several hours in cold water, drained and grated)
½ teaspoon salt
½ cup sour cream
2 eggs, separated

In mixing bowl, place drained grated potato, cream and salt. Beat egg yolks well and add to potato. Beat egg white stiffly and fold into mixture. Drop by spoonfuls on to a hot, well greased skillet. Turn cakes and brown slowly on both sides.

To serve pancakes as an appetizer-- top with sour cream and serve with apple sauce.

Whipped Carrots in Orange Cups

Serves 4

2 large oranges, juiced
1 large bag baby carrots (4 portions)
¼ to ½ cup heavy cream
¼ pound butter
Salt and pepper
Brown sugar to taste
Mint leaves or parsley for decoration

Cut orange sections in half and juice, reserving the shell
Add some sugar to a large pot of boiling water. Cook carrots and boil, until sharp knife goes in easily. Drain and place in food processor. Add butter, salt and pepper and a pinch of brown sugar and heavy cream, little at a time Taste and adjust the seasonings.
When ready to serve, fill the orange cups with the carrot puree. Cover with plastic wrap and microwave briefly to heat. Decorate with mint leaves or parsley.

Note-- whipped carrots may be made several days ahead and stored in the refrigerator and reheated when ready to serve. For less formal occasions, eliminate the orange sections and serve in a casserole

Frenched String Beans or Petite String Beans

Serves 4

1 pound string beans, Frenched, or petite beans
¼ cup butter
Garlic salt

Using a bean frencher, or a sharp knife, remove outside bean strings, and slice bean into thin strips.

In a fry pan, melt butter. Add beans and sprinkle liberally with garlic salt. Fry until browned. Serve immediately.

afternoon delight

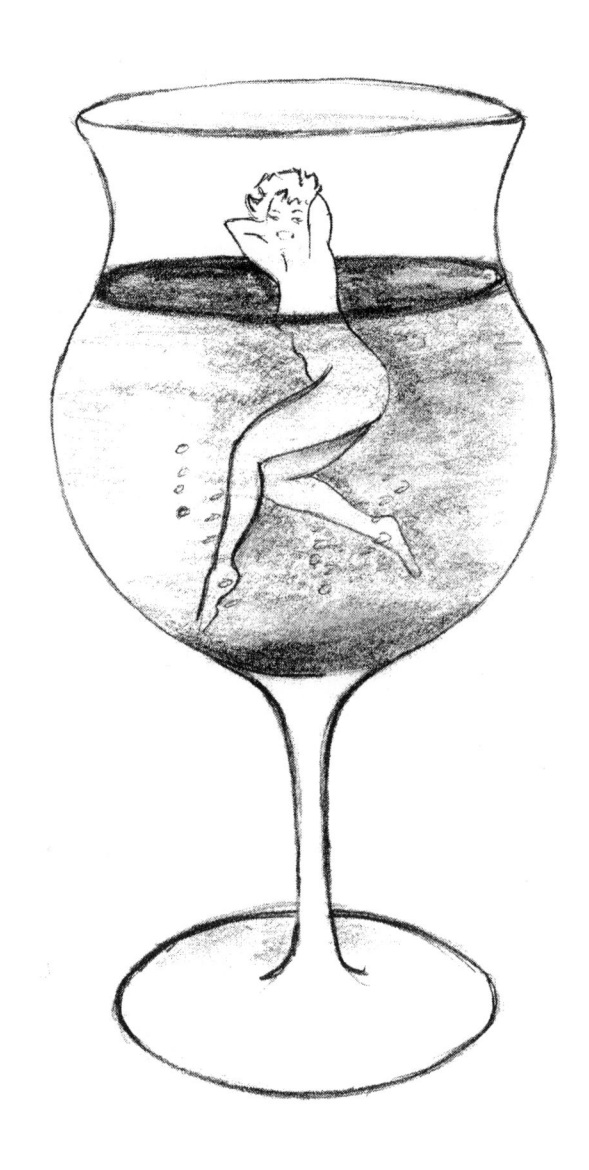

Non-Alcoholic Toddy

3 tea bags
2 cups boiling water
2 cups pure premium orange juice
1 teaspoon rum flavoring or almond extract
¼ cup confectioners' sugar
Low-fat vanilla frozen yogurt for garnish
Toasted sliced almonds for garnish

Bring the water to a boil in a 2-quart saucepan. Add the tea bags and let them steep covered for 5 minutes. Remove the tea bags and add the orange juice, rum flavoring, or almond extract and confectioners' sugar. Simmer the mixture over medium heat for 5 minutes. Pour the toddy into a tall glass with 1 tablespoon vanilla frozen yogurt and a teaspoon of sliced almonds.

Homemade Irish Cream

3 cups Brandy
2 eggs, well beaten
1 cup ½ and ½
1 - 14 ounce can Eagle brand milk
1 Tablespoon vanilla
1 Tablespoon Hershey brand chocolate syrup
1 ounce Kaluha or Tia Maria

Blend the above ingredients together and serve in a chilled glass or over ice.

Chocolate Raspberry Saddle Shoes

1 ounce raspberry liqueur
8 ounces cranberry juice cocktail or raspberry-cranberry drink
Whipped cream for garnish
Chocolate sprinkles for garnish
Maraschino cherry or fresh raspberry for garnish

Put all ingredients except garnishes in blender and blend on high speed for a few seconds or until all ingredients are mixed. Serve in a tall glass and garnish with whipped cream, chocolate sprinkles and cherry or raspberry

Cocoquito

2 - 12 ounce cans evaporated milk
1 – 15 ounce can cream of coconut (Goya brand) divided
1 – 14 ounce can condensed milk
1 to 2 teaspoons vanilla, to taste
1 egg yolk
Rum, to taste
Cinnamon

Add egg yolk, 1 can evaporated milk, ½ can cream of coconut, ½ can condensed milk and ½ of vanilla to blender and blend until smooth. Pour mixture into large container and sprinkle with cinnamon. Add rest of ingredients to blender and blend. Add to container and sprinkle with cinnamon. Blend all together and refrigerate for 24 hours. Pour into glass container (wine decanter) and serve.

Egg Nog

12 eggs, separated and at room temperature
6 cups milk
2 cups heavy cream
1 ½ cups sugar
2 cups bourbon plus ¾ cups brandy, or 2 ¾ cups dark Meyers Rum
2 teaspoons nutmeg
Vanilla ice cream

In a large mixing beat egg yolks until thick and lemon color. Add sugar and continue beating for about 10 minutes or until mixture is very thick and turns the color of butter. Add liquor a little at a time, (bourbon, brandy, or dark rum) cool and refrigerate for up to 6 hours before serving. 1/2 hour before your guests arrive, stir milk into chilled yolk mixture. Add 1 to 1/12 teaspoons nutmeg.

Place a separate bowl in the freezer along with clean electric beaters, until cold. Remove from freezer and pour chilled cream into cold bowl and beat on high until stiff peaks form.
In a separate bowl.

In a separate bowl, beat room temperature egg whites until stiff peaks form.

In a large punch bowl, gently fold egg white mixture into egg yolk mixture and hen fold in whipped cream.

Paradise Found

5 ounces pink grapefruit juice cocktail
2 ounces pineapple juice

Pour grapefruit juice and pineapple juice into a tall glass with ice. Top with lemon-lime soda. Garnish with orange juice.

Punch For All Occasions

Serves 20 to 25

40 ounces of raspberry juice
12 ounces frozen pineapple orange juice
2 liters 7 up or ginger ale
½ gallon frozen raspberry sherbet
½ gallon frozen pineapple sherbet
Decorative frozen ice ring molds
Rum, to taste (optional)

Combine all ingredients in a large punch bowl, adding the ginger ale at the last minute. Add ice rings and serve.

Park Avenue Punch

6 ounces raspberry-cranberry drink
1 ounce orange juice
¼ teaspoon lime juice
Club soda or sodium-free seltzer
Lime slice for garnish

Pour raspberry-cranberry drink, orange juice and lime juice in a tall glass filled with ice. Top with soda or seltzer. Garnish with lime slice.

White Punch

Serves 40

1 can frozen lemonade, 12 ounces
½ gallon white grape juice, white wine, or champagne
2 liters ginger ale
Decorative frozen ice rings

Mix frozen lemonade and grape juice in a large punch bowl. Add frozen ice rings. Pour in ginger ale at the last minute.

The Perfect Frozen Margarita

1 can frozen Margarita mix
Jose Cuervo Gold tequila, to top of empty Margarita mix can
Jose Cuervo liquid Margarita mix, to top of empty Margarita mix can
Juice if 1 fresh lime
Chopped ice
Fresh or frozen fruit, optional (strawberries, raspberries, peach, mango)
Smoothie machine or strong drink blender

Open one end of frozen Margarita can and put the frozen mixture into the smoothie top. Fill empty can with tequila and Add to smoothie top. Fill empty can with liquid Margarita mix and add to rest of the mixture. Add lime juice, fruit (optional), fill with ice and blend till smooth. Adjust ingredients and ice to taste. Serve immediately in salt rimmed Margarita glasses. Freeze any leftovers until ready to use.

Frozen Margaritas may be made several days ahead, in batches, and frozen until ready to serve. If you are tailgating, keep frozen mixture in a plastic bag, place in an insulated cooler and surround with ice and cold packs. Mixture will need stirring before pouring, so remember to include a long metal or wooden spoon.

The Big Orange

1 can frozen orange juice (do not add water)
Vodka, filled to top of empty frozen orange juice container)
Cream, milk, ½ and ½, or non-fat ½ and ½, filled to top of empty frozen orange juice container
1 Tablespoon real mayonnaise
Chopped ice

Place all ingredients in a smoothie machine or drink blender, and puree until smooth. Adjust ingredients to taste and serve.

Note-- drinks can be made in batches and frozen until ready to use. If tailgating (see **"Frozen Margaritas"**)

Mocha Brandy Frozen Drink Dessert

Coffee ice cream, softened
Brandy
Chocolate syrup
Rolled cookies (optional)

Place ice cream in smoothie machine or drink blender. Add brandy and chocolate syrup to taste, and blend. Pour into glass goblets, decorate with rolled cookie and serve immediately.

***Note*--** if you keep these items on hand, you will always have an excellent, quick dessert.

A blonde gets on a plane bound for Pittsburgh, but mistakenly sits in first class.
The stewardess approaches her and asks to see her ticket.
She tells the lady that she does not have a first class ticket and that she needs to sit in tourist class.
The blonde turns to the stewardess and exclaims "I'm blonde, I'm beautiful, and I'm going to Pittsburgh!
The stewardess, very politely shows the woman that her ticket is not for first class and that she must take her belongings and go through the cabin curtains and find a seat in tourist.
The blonde again exclaims "I'm blonde, I'm beautiful, and I'm going to Pittsburgh.
The exasperated stwardess goes to the Captain and explains the situation.
The Captain says he"ll take care of it and he goes to the blonde and whispers in her ear. The blonde picks up all her things, and very quickly goes into the tourist section.
The amazed stwardess goes to the Captain and asks how he got the stuborn blonde to move?
The Captain explains that he simply told her "First class wasn't going to Pittsburgh!

Let's See Some Cheesecake

Best Cheesecake Ever

Preheat oven 350
Serves 12

Crust
1 box Zwieback baby biscuits (baby aisle of any grocery store)
1 cup sugar
1 Tablespoon cinnamon
¼ pound butter (1 stick), melted
Pam

Grate biscuits in food processor, and add melted butter and cinnamon. Press onto bottom and sides of greased (with Pam) spring form. Place in freezer for a few minutes to set.

Filling
32 ounces of cream cheese, at room temperature
5 eggs
1 ¼ cups sugar
2 teaspoons vanilla
1 Tablespoon lemon juice

***Note*--** for Key Lime cheese cake, substitute key lime juice for lemon juice)

Place above mixture in a large bowl, and beat until smooth. Pour over crust mixture in spring form and bake at 350 degrees for 20 to 30 minutes, until set, but not browned. Remove from oven for 15 minutes. After 13 minutes, raise oven temperature to 475 degrees for 2 minutes.

Topping
2 cups sour cream
¼ cup sugar
1 teaspoon vanilla
1 box or bag of frozen strawberries, in light syrup, defrosted

Place sour cream, sugar, and vanilla, in a small and mix together with a spoon. Two minutes before returning cheesecake to the oven, carefully spoon topping over partially baked cheesecake. Return to oven for 7 to 10 minutes. Do not allow to brown. Remove from oven and cool before refrigerating. Cheesecake may be made four days ahead, and refrigerated until you wish to serve it. Serve with strawberries in light syrup.

***Note*--** Individual cheesecakes, bake 325 degrees for 20 minutes. Turn oven off and bake an additional 20 minutes.

Differently Delicious Cheesecake

Preheat oven 325 to 350 degrees
Serves 12

Crust
1 box Zwieback baby biscuits (found on baby aisle of grocery store)
¼ pound butter (1 stick)
1 cup sugar
2 teaspoons cinnamon
Pam

Place all ingredients in food processor bowl, and process. Spray spring form with Pam and press crust into sides and bottom, making sure you have plenty of crust where the spring form comes apart. Place in freezer for a few minutes to set.

Filling
4 eggs
1 cup sugar
1½ pounds of small curd cottage cheese, or farmers cheese
½ pint heavy cream
¼ cup flour
Juice of 1 large lemon
Pinch of salt
1 teaspoon vanilla
1 box frozen strawberries, or raspberries, packed in light syrup (optional: defrosted)

In a large bowl, beat eggs and salt until foamy. Add sugar and continue to beat until mixture is very thick, about 3 minutes. Alternately add the cream and the cheese and mix until thoroughly blended. Stir in the lemon juice and vanilla.

Fold in flour. Place a large coarse strainer or coarse sieve over a large bowl. Pour cheesecake mixture into the sieve and using a wooden spoon, rub the mixture through the sieve. The mixture is now very smooth and creamy. Pour into crust lined spring form and bake at 350 degrees for 1 hour or more. Cake should be firm.

Remove from oven and allow cooling thoroughly before refrigerating.

When ready to serve, run a knife around side edges of spring form before releasing. Cake may be stored up to 4 days in the refrigerator.

Little Bites Cheesecakes

Preheat oven to 350 degrees

¼ pound butter, melted
⅓ cup sugar
1 box Graham cracker crumbs or Oreo crumbs or Vanilla wafer crumbs, or Zwieback crumbs
4 eggs
1 cup sugar
4 (8-ounce) packages cream cheese, softened
Sour cream filling

Combine crumbs with butter and sugar until mixed. Spray mini muffin tins with Pam. Fill tins with paper liners Pack crumbs, using your finger or back of spoon.

Place eggs, sugar and cream cheese in a mixing bowl and cream until smooth. Spoon this mixture into tins, filling ¾ full.

Bake at 350 degrees for 15 to 20 minutes. Cool 10 to 15 minutes. Centers will fall. Carefully remove from tins and spoon 1 teaspoon of sour cream filling into each indentation.

Sour Cream Filling
1 8-ounce carton sour cream
¾ cup sugar
½ teaspoon vanilla extract

For color, especially at Christmas, cut maraschino cherries in quarters and top cake to look like a poinsettia. Mini cheese cakes are delicious with different toppings, such as blueberries, strawberries, chocolate chips, pecans, cherry pie filling or glaze strawberry with store bought strawberry glaze.

A farmer and his wife are in bed. He reaches over and fondles her breasts. "If these would only give milk, we could get rid of the cows".He moves his hand lower and says "if these would produce eggs, we could get rid of the chickens".

She reaches for his penis and says" if this would just get hard, we could get rid of your brother"

New York Cheesecake

Preheat oven to 400 degrees
Serves 12

Cookie Dough Crust
1 cup all purpose flour, sifted
¼ cup sugar
Grated rind of 1 lemon (see "Helps") or equal amount of lemon zest
1 egg yolk
½ cup butter, softened
¼ teaspoon vanilla
Additional soft butter for greasing sides of spring form

Use dough blade in food processor, and process flour, sugar, grated lemon rind, egg yoke, butter, and vanilla, until ball forms. Remove from food processor bowl, and wrap in plastic wrap. Refrigerate dough until chilled. Release the sides of the spring form, so that you can separate the sides from the bottom.

Roll 1/3 of dough to cover bottom of 9 inch spring form. Bake pie in preheated oven 400 degrees for 8 minutes. Remove from oven.

Butter sides of spring form and put baked crust covered bottom inside it and refasten the spring to close the spring form. Cool.

Roll remaining dough into 2 strips, 2 ½ inches wide and 14 inches long. Press into spring form sides.

Filling
40 ounces cream cheese (NOT nonfat or low fat)
1¾ cups sugar
3 Tablespoons all purpose flour
¼ teaspoon salt
Grated rind of 1 lemon (see "Helps") or equivalent lemon zest
Grated rind ½ orange (see "Helps") or equivalent orange zest
5 eggs
2 egg yolks
¼ cup heavy cream
¼ teaspoon vanilla

To assemble
While you are making the cookie dough crust, bring the filling ingredients to room temperature (eggs, butter, and cream cheese). Place cream cheese in large bowl and beat until soft.

continued

Sift together, the sugar, flour and the salt. Gradually blend mixture into the cream cheese, keeping the mixture smooth. Add grated rinds. Add eggs, one at a time, beating thoroughly after each addition. Blend in cream.

Pour into crusted spring form pan, and bake in preheated oven at 475 degrees for 15 minutes. Without opening the oven door, reduce the oven temperature to 225 degrees and continue to bake for an additional 1 hour and then, without opening the oven door, turn oven temperature off and leave the cake in the oven for an additional 15 minutes.

Remove cheesecake from oven and cool on a cake rack, away from a draft. When cool, refrigerate. Cheesecake can be made up to four days ahead and refrigerated until ready to use. Left over cheesecake will store in the refrigerator for several days, but I doubt you will have any leftovers.

Decorating
It is not necessary to decorate a cheesecake. It's delicious served with defrosted strawberries, or raspberries, frozen in light syrup. Serve in a gravy boat, allowing guests to spoon berries and syrup on top of their cheesecake, if they wish. To glaze the cheesecake, top with large fresh strawberries, pointed end up. Spoon store bought glaze (or make your own), over top of berries. For 4th of July celebration, make an American flag out of fresh raspberries and fresh blueberries, or stick a long birthday candle with fresh blueberries pushed through to cover the candle, exposing candle wick for lighting,

The King of India finds himself in Las Vegas, tapped out of money. He notices a Pawn Shop across the street. He figures he can pawn "The Star of India Diamond".
He asks the Pawn broker "How much for this huge diamond?"
The Pawn broker offers him very little money, even though the stone is huge.
"Do you realize who you are talking to?" the King asks.
The Pawn broker turns the diamond over in his hand and sings "When you wish upon a star, makes no difference who you are!"

Ricotta Cheesecake

Preheat oven 325 degrees

Crust
1 ½ cups graham cracker crumbs
6 Tablespoons butter, melted
¼ cup granulated sugar
1 teaspoon grated lemon rind
1 teaspoon nutmeg
1 teaspoon cinnamon

Place ingredients in a mixing bowl and blend. Remove ring from spring form and cover bottom with parchment paper. Grease 9 inch spring form, bottom and sides and pack with crumb mixture making sure that the crumbs are packed tightly in the corners where the spring form will be removed. Place in freezer to set.

Filling
4 cups ricotta cheese
½ cup sugar
4 eggs, lightly beaten
1 Tablespoon cornstarch
1 teaspoon almond extract
1 cup heavy cream
½ cup almonds, finely chopped

Place ricotta cheese in a strainer and drain all the liquid.

In a large mixing bowl, beat ricotta with sugar until light and fluffy. Add beaten eggs, cornstarch and almond extract. Stir in cream and nuts, and pour into cookie lined spring form.

Bake at 325 degrees for 1 hour or longer if necessary. Turn oven to off, but leave cake in oven with the *oven door open*, to cool to room temperature. Refrigerate up to 4 days.

Secret Cheesecake Recipe

Preheat oven 325
Serves 12

Crust
1 box graham crackers crumb
½ cup butter (1 stick), melted
Pam

If graham crackers are not crushed, place in food processor and pulse until you have graham cracker crumbs. Spray Pam on sides and bottom of spring form. Add melted butter and mix into crumbs. Pack crumbs into the bottom and sides of the spring form, pressing with your hands and fingers. Put cookie lined spring form in the freezer to set.

Filling
5 eggs, well beaten
Dash of salt
2 cups sugar
16 ounces sour cream
32 ounces of cream cheese (4 8 ounce packages), room temperature
1 ounce lemon juice or ½ of a fresh lemon, remove pits
1 teaspoon vanilla

Beat eggs, with a dash of salt, until lemon in color. Beat in lemon juice, softened cream cheese, sugar, and sour cream. Beat until smooth. Pour into crusted spring form and bake in oven at 325 degrees for 1 hour. Turn oven temperature off and leave cheese cake in the oven for an additional 1 hour. Do not open oven door.

Chill in refrigerator for several hours and up to four days. Loosen sides of spring form with a sharp knife. Release spring and remove cheese cake, leaving the bottom of the spring form under the cake.

A little boy sits down on the bus next to a priest. He stares at the man and finally asks,
"Why do you wear your collar backwards?"
"I am the father of many", the priests replies.
"My daddy has four children and fifteen grand children and he does not wear his collar backwards."
"Well I am the father of hundreds" says the priest.
The little boy thinks for a few minutes and says "Maybe you should wear your pants backwards."

yummy nummies

Brownies - Regular or Mint

Preheat oven to 350 degrees

½ pound butter
4 ounces unsweetened chocolate
4 eggs
2 cups of sugar
½ cup flour
1 teaspoon vanilla
⅔ cup walnuts, pecans, or macadamia nuts
Andes candies, shaved Hershey bar, or milk chocolate chips or white chocolate
Frosting, canned or homemade
Powdered sugar (optional)

Prepare 9x12 pan. Spray with Pam, line with parchment paper, and re-spray. Melt butter and unsweetened chocolate in double boiler or microwave and set aside. In separate bowl, beat eggs and sugar until thick and lemony. Add vanilla. Fold melted chocolate mixture into eggs and sugar mixture. Mix thoroughly. Sift flour and fold into mixture. Fold in chopped nuts.

Spread ½ mixtures into prepared pan and spread Andes mints (or choice of chocolates) on top; then top with remaining mixture.

Note-- for non-mint brownies, add ⅓ largest slivered Hershey bar, or milk chocolate chips, instead of mints. Instead of icing, sift powdered sugar over lace doily that has been placed on top of brownies. Lift doily and a pretty sugar pattern will appear. Use pizza cutter to slice.

Bake at 350 degrees for 25 minutes, or until edges start to pull away from the sides of the pan. Remove from oven and cool for 30 minutes. Store or freeze. It is easier to frost brownies after partially defrosted. Cut into squares and serve.

Velvety Brownie Icing
6 ounces semi-sweet chocolate
¼ cup strong coffee, brewed
1 cup butter
¾ cup corn syrup
4 egg yolks

Melt chocolate and coffee in double boiler. Cream butter and beat into chocolate mixture. Set aside. In a heavy pan, bring corn syrup to a boil. Cook until corn syrup spins like a thread when a spoon of the syrup is lifted high. Beat egg yolks until thick, and then beat in corn syrup. Cool. Combine cooled chocolate mixture and cooled egg corn syrup mixture.

Chocolate Chewies

Preheat oven to 350 degrees
Makes 36 cookies

2-ounces (2 squares) unsweetened chocolate
6-ounces (6 squares) semi-sweet chocolate
2 Tablespoons butter
¼ cup sifted all-purpose flour
¼ teaspoon baking powder
⅛ teaspoon salt
2 eggs
¾ cups sugar
2 teaspoons instant coffee
½ teaspoon vanilla extract
6-ounces (1 cup) semi-sweet chocolate morsels
6-ounces chopped walnuts or pecans
Aluminum foil

Adjust rack ⅓ of the way down from the top of the oven. Preheat oven to 350 degrees.

Cut aluminum foil to fit cookie sheets. In the top of a small double boiler melt the unsweetened and semi-sweet chocolate squares and the butter over hot water on moderate heat. Stir until smooth. Remove top of double boiler and set aside to cool completely.

Stir together the flour, baking powder and salt. Set aside. In small bowl of electric mixer, beat eggs, sugar, coffee and vanilla at high speed for a minute or two.

On low speed, add the cooled chocolate and finally the sifted dry ingredients, scraping bowl as necessary to keep mixture smooth, and beating only until blended. Stir in the chocolate morsels and nuts.

Drop by heaping teaspoonfuls one-inch apart (these hardly spread at all) on the aluminum foil-lined cookie sheets. Bake 10 to 12 minutes at 350 degrees, reversing position of cookie sheet as necessary during baking to ensure even browning.

Tops will be dry, but centers should remain soft and chewy. DO NOT OVERBAKE.

It is best to let these stand or chill until chocolate morsels re-harden, before serving.

Ginger Creams

Preheat oven 325 degrees

½ cup butter
1 cup sugar
½ cup molasses
1 egg
3 cups sifted flour
1 teaspoon baking soda
1 teaspoon cinnamon
1 teaspoon ginger
1 teaspoon cloves
Salt
1 cup cold coffee

Combine the first 4 ingredients. Sift flour, baking soda, cinnamon, cloves, and salt. Add sifted ingredients to first 4 ingredients along with the coffee. Mix ingredients until creamy. Spread evenly over a large cookie sheet or cake tin. Bake 15-20 min and frost with carrot cake frosting or caramel frosting (see "NAUGHTY SAUCY")

Current Jelly Gems

Preheat oven to 375 degrees

2 sticks of butter (room temperature)
½ cup sugar
2 egg yolks
1 teaspoon vanilla
¼ teaspoon salt
2 cups of flour, sifted
2 egg whites
Chopped walnuts
Currant jelly

Blend the first 5 ingredients in a bowl. Then add sifted flour.

Form into small balls, and dip in egg whites, and roll in chopped walnuts. Place cookie balls on parchment paper lined cookie sheet. Using your thumb, make indentation in middle of cookies.

Bake in oven at 375 to 400 degrees for 20 to 25 minutes until brown. While still warm, put currant jelly in center indentation.

Hello Dollies

Preheat oven 325 degrees

1 cup graham cracker crumbs
½ cup butter, melted
1 cup coconut flakes
6 ounce package chocolate morsels
6 ounce package butterscotch morsels
15 ounces sweetened condensed milk
1½ cups nuts, chopped (pecans or walnuts)

Spray 7x11 (or any preferred sized) baking pan, with Pam. Alternately layer crumbs, butter, chocolate, butterscotch, nuts and milk. Bake 325 degrees, for 30 minutes. Loosen sides with a sharp knife and allow to cool. Cut into squares and remove from pan. Store in air tight container or freeze.

A man is ship wrecked on a deserted island. For years he spends every day fishing on the beach and searching the horizon for ships that might bring him back to civilization. One day, as he is fishing, he sees a gorgeous woman arise out of the water, wearing a wet suit that reveals a magnificent body. As she slowly walks out of the water towards him, he explains that he has been stranded there for a very long time. She asks if there is anything he has been dieing for, maybe she could provide it?
He thinks for a minute and says "You don't happen to have a cigarette do you?
With that, she unzips one of the wet suit pockets and produces a pack of Marlboros and a lighter.
He can't believe his good fortune as he takes a deep drag on the cigarette.
Once again she asks if there is anything else he has been dieing for?
"You don't happen to have a hamburger do you?"
With that she unzips another pocket and produces a double pounder with cheese. The man greedily gobbles down the hamburger.
The gal looks at him says "Would you like to play around?"
He replies "Don't tell me you also have golf clubs"?

Peanut Butter Chocolate Drops

Makes 8 dozen

2 cups crunchy peanut butter
¾ cup butter or margarine, softened
1 (1 pound) box powdered sugar
3 cups crisp rice cereal
1 (8-ounce) milk chocolate candy bar
1 (6-ounce) package semi-sweet chocolate morsels
½ (4-ounce) cake paraffin (available at grocery store canning aisle)

Cream peanut butter and butter. Add powdered sugar and beat until light and fluffy. Stir in cereal. Using your hands, roll mixture into 1-inch balls and place in freezer or refrigerator until chilled.
Melt milk chocolate, chocolate morsels and paraffin in a saucepan over low heat, stirring frequently. Dip each ball into chocolate mixture and place on waxed paper to harden. Once chocolate has hardened on the cookies, they can be packaged and frozen or stored in an airtight container.

***Note*-**- cookies are easiest to dip in chocolate, if you use tooth picks.

A distraught dog owner, lovingly carrying his very sick animal in his arms, walks into his vet's office and asks the doctor what is wrong with his dog. The doctor pronounces the dog dead. The man begins to cry and begs the doctor for a second opinion. The vet calls in his cat. The cat walks from one end of the dog to the other. He turns toward the Doctor and shakes his head. "I'm sorry, but the cat also thinks there is no hope for your pet. The dog owner just cannot accept their opinion, and begs for yet a 3rd consultation. The understanding Doctor tries to help and calls for his Labrador retriever. The dog jumps up on the examining table and sniffs the patient from one end to the other. He shakes his head, jumps off the table, and leaves the room. The Vet turns to the owner and sadly tells him that his dog is dead. A few weeks later, the Doctor gets a call from the dead dog's owner, and he is furious. "I got a bill from you for $650, just to tell me that my dog was dead. I think that charge is outrageous!" "Well, says the Vet, it was $50 for my diagnosis, but when you asked for a CAT SCAN and the LAB report, the price when up!"

Pecan Puffs

Preheat oven to 325 degrees
Makes 40 puffs

½ pound unsalted butter, softened
4 Tablespoons granulated sugar
2 teaspoons almond extract
2 cups cake flour (measure before sifting)
1 teaspoon vanilla
2 cups ground pecans (measure before grinding)
Powdered sugar
Parchment paper

Mix butter, granulated sugar, almond extract, cake flour, vanilla and pecans. Roll into balls.

Line heavy duty cookie sheet with ungreased parchment paper. Bake at 325 degrees for 20 to 25 minutes. While hot, roll twice in powdered sugar.

When baking, place a second four sided cookie sheet under pan that holds cookies. The air in between will help to keep the cookies from burning on the bottom.

A very well endowed woman goes to a plastic surgeon and asks him if he can perform a breast reduction on her.
He looks her over and asks if she would mind if he numbed her breasts first.
She said that would be fine and she proceeded to take of her sweater off and undo her bra.
The Doctor takes her huge breasts, one in each hand, and with his mouth he goes NUM NUM NUM NUM NUM!!!

Pecan Tassies

Preheat oven to 350 degrees
Makes 3 dozen

Crust
3 ounces cream cheese, room temperature
1 cup flour
¼ cup butter, room temperature

Blend the above ingredients in food processor, using a dough blade. Place a small ball of the pastry in a muffin tin heavily greased with Pam and press to line the tin. Make sure not to make the crust too thin on the bottom or filling will ooze out.

Filling
3 Tablespoons melted butter
3 eggs, slightly beaten
2 ¼ cups brown sugar
½ teaspoon salt
½ teaspoon vanilla
1½ cup chopped pecans

Mix thoroughly and fill crust lined tins. Bake at 350 degrees for 20 minutes. Remove from oven and immediately run a sharp knife or curved serrated grapefruit knife, around all edges, popping tassies out of muffin tins. Cool and store.

To freeze, place single layer in resealable freezer bags. Delicious as frozen snacks or defrosted as mini pecan pies. Wonderful topped with ice cream or sweetened whipped cream.

A couple has been married for 25 years. He asks how she would like to spend their anniversary. She says she would like to go to the same hotel, the same room, if possible, the same meal etc...
He makes the arrangements. As they enter the suite, she puts her arms around him and asks, "Do you remember what was on your mind 25 years ago?"
"Yes" he says, "I thought I would screw your brains out and suck your breasts dry"
"And today" she asks?
"I think I did a good job" he said.

happy endings

Bûche de Noël

Preheat oven to 450 degrees

4-sided cookie sheet
Parchment paper or waxed paper
7 jumbo eggs room temperature, separated
1½ cup powdered sugar, sift if lumpy
3 heaping tablespoons unsweetened cocoa
1 teaspoon vanilla
Pinch of salt
1 cup heavy cream, whipped and sweetened with powdered sugar
1 layer of brown paper, larger than cookie sheet
Decorators

Directions
Spray cookie sheet with Pam. Cover with parchment paper or waxed paper and mold into corners. Spray parchment paper entirely with Pam.

Beat egg yolks until lemon-yellow. Gradually add sugar and continue beating on high until VERY thick, about 5 to 10 minutes. Add cocoa and vanilla   Using clean beaters, add a pinch of salt, and beat egg whites until stiff. Using a wire whisk, fold ½ of the beaten egg whites into chocolate egg yolk mixture allowing for plenty of air. Carefully fold in the rest of the egg whites...

Spread mixture evenly in prepared cookie sheet. Bake at 450 degrees in the middle of the oven, 5 to 8 minutes. DO NOT BURN. To test for doneness, touch the top of chocolate roll. If your finger indentation springs back from the touch, roll is ready to remove from oven. If you feel that the center is still runny, return to oven for few minutes. Cool slightly.

To roll, lay a single layer of brown paper on top of Bûche de Noël and invert. Remove pan from roll and carefully peel off the parchment paper and discard. Roll in brown paper while warm, forming a chocolate log. Allow to cool completely (do not refrigerate)

Whip cream stiff and sweeten with powdered sugar to taste.

To unroll chocolate roll, carefully separate the brown paper from the roll. Spread with sweetened whipped cream and re-roll without the brown paper. Before frosting, trim ends with an electric knife. Frost log with Good Mocha Icing. Use ½ recipe for one chocolate roll. Decorate top and both ends of cake and refrigerate. Since the end pieces are the most popular, you can cut the roll in half and frost four ends, instead of only two.

Decorate for the holidays
Drag fork tines along brown frosting to create log texture. Use maraschino cherries that have been cut into quarters to create poinsettias. Draw leaves and stems with green decorating tube. Bûche de Noël can be filled with ice cream instead of whipped cream. Freeze; slice and serve with hot fudge sauce.

Good Mocha Icing

¼ cup vegetable shortening (Crisco)
2 teaspoons powdered instant coffee
⅛ teaspoon salt
½ teaspoon vanilla
2 cups confectioners' sugar (sift if lumpy)
1 small egg (or part of large egg)
⅛ to ¼ cup milk (add only enough for spreadable consistency)
¼ cup cocoa (non-sweetened)

Blend egg, cocoa, coffee, and salt. Add sugar alternately with vanilla and just enough milk to spread the frosting easily. You may not need any milk at all. Use ½ teaspoon of milk at a time.

Frost roll, including sides and ends. To decorate use fork tongs for log effect. This is especially appropriate for a Christmas dessert. Use maraschino cherries cut into fourths, and create poinsettias.

A Japanese, an American and Irishman find themselves sharing a Jacuzzi.
When the American's hand starts to ring he says "Excuse me, my phone is ringing" and he proceeds to answer his palm.
A few minutes later, the arm of the Japanese starts to ring. He excuses himself and explains that he had a pager chip surgically put into his arm.
Now the Irishman is feeling very "low tech". He leaves the Jacuzzi to go to the men's room. Upon his return, he finds the American and the Japanese snickering. When he asks what they are laughing at, they explain that he still has toilet paper coming out of his butt. Thinking quickly, he replies "Oh, I must be getting a fax".

Bread Pudding

Preheat oven to 350 degrees
Serves 6

12 ounces day old French bread
4 slices white bread, to be used later

Custard Sauce
5 whole eggs
1 egg yolk
1 Tablespoon vanilla
½ cup sugar
4 Tablespoons butter (¼ stick)
2 cups milk
1 cup heavy cream
2 cups raisins, sprinkled with a small amount of rum, and divided
4 Tablespoons cinnamon, divided
⅛ teaspoon nutmeg
Pam
1½ cup Whiskey Sauce (see below)

To make custard sauce, beat the eggs and sugar in a large mixing bowl, at medium speed. Add the milk, heavy cream, and blend. Reduce mixer speed to low speed. Blend in two tablespoons of cinnamon, nutmeg, and vanilla.

Cut the French bread into small slices. Lightly Pam a 9 inch cake pan, 2 inches deep. Sprinkle the bottom with 2 tablespoons of the remaining cinnamon and ⅔ cups of raisins. Spread a second layer of bread over the raisins and cover it with one-third of the custard mixture.

Make sure the custard soaks in completely by pressing the bread down with your hands, until all is absorbed. Repeat the sequence (cinnamon, raisins, bread, and custard) twice more, to produce three complete layers, in all. Top with the 4 loaf slices of white bread and press them down, to make sure the bread is soaked with the custard. Sprinkle with additional cinnamon, if desired. Bake for 1 hour at 350 degrees. Serve warm, topped with 4 tablespoons of warm whiskey sauce per portion.

Butterscotch Bread Pudding

Preheat oven 350 degrees

Follow bread pudding recipe, except use brioche instead of French bread. Break brioche into pieces and place in buttered individual ramekins, layering the bread with butterscotch morsels. Add custard recipe, and seasonings following recipe from above. Push the custard into the bread, until all the custard is soaked into the brioche pieces. Bake at 350 degrees until done. The time depends on the size of the individual ramekins.

Bread Pudding Whiskey Sauce

3 eggs
2 sticks of butter, melted and cooled
½ cup powdered sugar
1½ teaspoons bourbon

Beat eggs until frothy. Slowly add cooled, melted or softened butter. Slowly beat in powdered sugar. Add bourbon to taste. Serve over bread pudding. Mixture will not separate, if it is made in the food processor.

A man is walking down the Malibu beach, when thunder rolls and lighting strikes. The man hears the voice of God saying "My son, you have been such a good person, I would like to reward you. Ask me for anything. So the man asks for a bridge from Malibu to Hawaii. God replies "Do you realize how many steel supports would be needed and how much cement it would take, to say nothing about how hard it would be to design. Can't you think of any other request?" The man thinks and replies "Well my wife is always complaining that I don't understand her. Can you help me to understand women?" God thinks for a minute and says "Now, would you like that road one lane or two?

Brownie Ice Cream Sandwich

Preheat oven 350 degrees
Serves 8

1 box brownie mix or (see '"YUMMY NUMMIES" for home made brownie mixture)
Chopped nuts (optional)
Ice cream, one or two flavored, softened
Frosting (homemade or canned) or sweetened whipped cream
Desired toppings
Parchment paper
Pam

Spray cookie sheet with Pam and line with parchment paper. Follow package directions, (or home made brownie recipe) and spread brownie mixture very thinly over parchment paper. Bake only until brownie is done but be careful not to burn mixture. Remove from oven and cut into three equal pieces. Allow to cool. Working very quickly, spread ice cream on top of first brownie section. Place second brownie section on top of ice cream and add more ice cream, switching flavors if desired. Place last brownie section on top of ice cream and place in freezer. Freeze until ice cream hardens. Remove from freezer and quickly frost.

***Note*--** it is not necessary to frost. Sandwich can be sliced and served with toppings on the side. Wrap frozen mixture in plastic wrap and aluminum foil. Return to freezer. Slice only what you need, and return leftovers to freezer. You will always have an excellent dessert on hand for last minute emergencies.

A nurse is walking down the hall of an old age home. One of the male patients grabs her arm and says, "did you know that my penis died today?"
"That's terrible", she replies.
The next day, she sees him walking down the hall with his penis flapping in the breeze and says to him, "I thought your penis died"?
"It did" says the old man, "today's the viewing!"

Angel Food Cake with Caramel Frosting

Preheat oven according to box directions

1 Angel food cake mix
1 tube pan, not greased

Bake Angel food cake following box directions, or buy an Angel food cake at the bakery that is not iced.

Caramel frosting

1½ cups brown sugar
¾ cup cream
2 Tablespoons butter
½ teaspoon vanilla

Boil sugar and cream until a soft ball forms when a small amount of hot icing is dropped into cold water. Add butter and vanilla. Spread over top of Angel Food cake, allowing frosting, to run down the sides and tube center. Using a spatula or knife, smooth frosting until all cake is iced, or just let icing run down the sides of the cake.

A husband and wife have been married for 25 years. He asks her how she would like to spend their anniversary. She says she would like to go back to the same hotel they spent their honeymoon in and preferably the same room. The husband makes all the arrangements. After he tips the bell hop for carrying their luggage to the suite, he asks his wife of 25 years what she would like to do next. She asks if he remembers their mad love scene, where they went into separate rooms, undressed, and at a given signal they rushed into each others arms. He agrees to reenact and off they go to separately rooms to undress. At a given signal they rush into each others arms, except they miss and he goes flying out the window. He now finds himself several stories below and naked. He beckons to a bell hop "can you get me a robe?" The bell hop says it won't be necessary, Sir. "I cannot walk through the lobby naked" the husband says "yes you can" the bell hop says" there is no one in the lobby, they are all upstairs trying to get some fool woman off the door knob."

Chocolate Bavarian Pie

Serves 6 to 8

3 slightly beaten egg yolks
½ cup sugar
¼ teaspoon salt
1 cup milk, scalded
1 envelope unflavored gelatin
¼ cup cold water
1 teaspoon vanilla
3 egg whites at room temperature
1 cup heavy cream, whipped
⅓ cup melted butter
1 box very thin chocolate wafers

Microwave or boil milk, until a skin forms on the top.

In the top of double boiler, combine egg yolks, sugar and salt. Slowly add milk. Have water in bottom of double boiler at simmer. Cook until mixture coats spoon, but do not allow to curdle..

Soften gelatin in cold water for five minutes. When set, stir into hot milk, egg and sugar mixture. Chill until partially set. Add vanilla.

Beat egg whites until stiff, but not dry.

Place heavy cream, electric beaters and a bowl in the freezer until chilled, before beating.

Fold beaten egg whites into whipped cream. Pour into chocolate wafer crust. Sprinkle top with ¼ cup wafer crumbs. Chill.

Make chocolate wafer crust
In food processor bowl, using metal blade, combine 1¼ cups chocolate wafer with ⅓ cup melted butter. Process until cookies becomes crumbs and set aside. Reserve ¼ cup crumbs for top, press remaining crumbs firmly in buttered 9" deep-dish prepared pan. Chill until set. Top with reserved crumbs.

Chocolate Chip Cake

Preheat oven to 350 degrees

1 package Duncan Hines Yellow cake mix
1 package vanilla instant pudding
1 cup vegetable oil
4 eggs
1 cup milk
1 - 8 ounce chocolate bar, grated
8 ounces chocolate chips

Combine above ingredients, except for chocolate. When blended, fold in 1 bar semi-sweet chocolate, grated, and 6 to 8 ounces chocolate chips, ungrated.

Pour into well greased and floured bundt pan.

Bake at 350 degrees for 50 to 60 minutes.

A woman wakes up one morning and finds a green rash between her legs. She goes in to see her gynecologist. Not knowing what the rash is, he sends her to a dermatologist. The skin doctor is puzzled and sends her to the Mayo Clinic. She is under observation for a week when a team of 5 doctors admit that they cannot figure it out and suggest she sees a Guru on the top of a mountain in San Jose, California.
So she gets on a flight to San Jose, finds the Guru's house and climbs up the many steps and knocks on the big wooden door.
The Guru opens the door and ushers the woman inside. She explains her malady and shows him the green rash inside of her thighs.
The Guru strokes the beard on his chin and pronounces "ah ha, ah hum, ah ha... you have a Gypsy lover?"
"How did you know" she exclaims.
"Tell him his ear rings are not REAL GOLD".

Chocolate Soufflé

Preheat oven to 375 degrees
Makes 4 to 6 servings

3 Tablespoons butter
3 Tablespoons flour
1¼ cups half and half
¼ cup very strong coffee
6 ounces semi-sweet chocolate
½ teaspoon vanilla
3 Tablespoons sugar
4 egg yolks
6 egg whites at room temperature
1 Tablespoon sugar
6 Tablespoons softened butter
6 Tablespoons sugar
¼ teaspoon cream of tartar
Pinch of salt

White Sauce
Melt 3 tablespoons butter. Add flour all at once. Stir and continue to cook over medium heat for one minute. This will eliminate the taste of flour. Heat half and half in microwave until scalded (skin forms on top). Make a roux by adding hot half and half, a little at a time to the flour mixture, stirring until smooth. As mixture thickens, add coffee. Keep stirring. Add chocolate chips and stir until melted forming a chocolate white sauce. Set aside.

Beat 4 egg yolks until lemon yellow. Add 3 tablespoons sugar and continue beating until very thick (when beaters are lifted from mixture, the eggs will fall back into the bowl in a ribbon. Add a small amount of white sauce to egg yolk mixture to warm it. Then add beaten yolk mixture to white sauce. Cool. Add vanilla. This can be prepared early.

Prepare Soufflé Dish and Collar
Heavily grease a six-cup soufflé mold (or individual ramekins) with 2 tablespoons of softened butter. Pour 2 to 3 tablespoons of sugar into the mold, covering all the surfaces. Shake mold and discard excess sugar. This step can be done several days ahead and refrigerated.

If you lack a soufflé, use a straight-sided baking dish. To add height, fold a double strip of buttered and sugared foil (butter side facing in) in half and wrap around the dish forming a collar that stands about 3 inches above soufflé dish. Overlap foil and secure with tape. This step can be done several days ahead.

Beating and folding makes all the difference
The lightness of any soufflé depends largely on how stiffly the egg whites have been beaten and how gently they have been folded into the body of the soufflé.

One hour before serving, beat 6 egg whites until foamy. If a copper bowl is not available, use any material except aluminum. Add a pinch of salt and ¼ teaspoon cream of tartar. Continue beating until stiff but not dry. The last minute of beating, add 1 tablespoon of sugar.

Using a wire whisk, gently fold ¼ of beaten egg white mixture into the cooled chocolate mixture, incorporating plenty of air. Fold in the rest of the egg white, until whites are no longer visible. Carefully pour the mixture into a soufflé mold, filling to within 2 inches from the top. Smooth the top with spatula. To form a cap, put a knife edge 1 inch into the mixture and draw a circle.

Set the soufflé dish into a larger pan. Add enough hot water to the bottom pan to go 1/3 up the sides of the pan. Bake at 375 degrees for 45 to 50 minutes (15 minutes less baking time for individual soufflés). To prevent soufflé from falling, walk softly and don't bang anything. Do not open the oven door until all baking time has elapsed…

Ice Cream Sauce
½ gallon vanilla ice cream
½ pint heavy cream, whipped

Soften ice cream and stir in whipped heavy cream. Refreeze. Remove from freezer shortly before serving.

Eat Immediately!!

Question:
What's the difference between a Jewish American Princess and an Italian Princess?

Answer:
An Italian Princess has fake jewelry and real orgasms.

Crème Brûlée

Preheat oven to 300 degrees

2 cups heavy cream
3 tablespoon sugar
4 egg yolks, beaten
1 teaspoon vanilla
1 teaspoon brandy or Cognac
Pam

Topping
½ cup dark brown sugar, sifted

Place cream in a heavy pan and boil until skin appears (scald). Add sugar and dissolve, but do not allow mixture to boil.

In a separate bowl, beat the egg yolks until thick and yellow. Slowly, stirring constantly, add the cream mixture to the beaten egg yolks, adding a little of the hot mixture first to warm the eggs, so they will not cook when the hot cream is added. Add vanilla and brandy.

Grease a 1 ½ quart baking dish and fill with custard mixture. Place dish inside a baking container that holds 2 inches of hot water.

Bake at 300 degrees for 45 to 50 minutes or until knife comes out clean. Cover and cool.

To serve
Sprinkle top of custard with the brown sugar and set dish in a pan of ice cubes. Place under broiler just long enough for sugar to melt, but do not allow to burn, so watch carefully. You may use a Brûlée torch instead of broiling the sugar to form the sugar crust topping you desire.

A couple is extremely competitive. One day they go to play golf and in the middle of the round, the guy says "I have to go into the woods and pee." The gal also has to go, so they both go into the woods. She says "I'll bet I can pee higher up on that tree than you can." So they make a bet. She pulls down her golf skirt and her panties and sidles up as high on the tree trunk as she can possibly get to leave her water mark. The guy laughs, confident that he will indeed be the easy winner. As he undoes his belt, and pulls down his fly, she says "NO HANDS!"

Dessert Crepe

Basic Crepe Batter (see "Breakfast in Bed")
Makes about 10 crepes

Apple Crepes
Granny Smith apples, peeled and sliced thin
Cinnamon
Sugar
Apple butter or apple jelly
Walnuts, chopped
Maple syrup
Prepared crepes

Marinate apples briefly in cinnamon and sugar. Cover with saran and microwave on high until apples are soft. .Cover cooked crepe and microwave on high, briefly, until crepe is warm. Open crepe flat and spread with a little apple butter in center and fill with softened apples. Mix walnuts and maple syrup, cover and warm in microwave. Pour on top of apple filled crepes.

Strawberry Filled Crepes
Fresh strawberries, sliced
Triple Sec liqueur or liqueur of choice
Strawberry jam or jelly
Sliced almonds, toasted (see "HOT NUTS")
Whipped cream, sweetened
Prepared crepes

Marinate strawberries in liqueur, briefly.

Warm crepe in microwave (see above) Open crepe flat and spread with a little jam. Top with strawberries. Roll crepe and top with sweetened whipped cream or vanilla ice cream and nuts.

Banana Crepes
Sliced bananas
Toasted Almonds (see "HOT NUTS")
Sweet vermouth
Light brown sugar
Whipped cream, sweetened
Apricot jam or jelly
Prepared crepe

continued

In a small bowl, place some brown sugar and stir in a little sweet vermouth until you have created a smooth sauce. Add bananas and marinate briefly.

Warm crepe (see above directions) Open crepe flat and spread a little jam, down the center. Top with bananas and roll crepe. Top with sweetened whipped cream.

Chocolate Crepes
Vanilla or chocolate ice cream
Chocolate sauce, warmed
Nuts, chopped
Whipped cream, sweetened
Cooked crepe

Warm crepe, following directions above. Open crepe flat and fill with ice cream, roll and top with sweetened whipped cream, chocolate sauce, and nuts. Serve immediately.

A 65 year old accountant is feuding with his 60 year old wife. One morning she comes down to breakfast and finds a note from him which said " I am having an affair with my 20 year old secretary, do not wait dinner!"
When the husband comes home that night he finds a note from his wife that reads
" I am having an affair with our 20 year old pool guy, and as you know, 20 goes into 60 a lot more times than 65 goes into 20, so don't wait up!"

Floating Island with Caramel Drizzle

Serves 6

To make Meringues
6 egg whites, room temperature
1 cup sugar
⅛ teaspoon salt

Beat egg whites with a dash of salt. When egg whites are no longer foamy, add ¾ cups of sugar, and beat until egg whites form a stiff peak when beaters are raised. Add the remaining ¼ cups of sugar and let stand for a few minutes (see "HELPS") and beat in.

To poach meringues, fill large fry pan ¾ full of water or milk. Heat to 170 degrees (do NOT allow to boil) Using an ice cream scoop; drop snow eggs onto the hot liquid and allow eggs to get firm. Remove with slotted spoon and drain on paper towels. Snow eggs should be firm and hold their shape as meringues islands.

To make Cream an glace or Custard Sauce
(see "NAUGHTY SAUCY")

To assemble
Place custard sauce in individual dessert dishes. Float the meringue islands on top of crème a glace, and drizzle a thin stream of caramel over each meringue egg.

To make Caramelized Dribble
1 cup sugar
5 Tablespoons water

Place water and sugar in a fry pan. Cook over high heat, without stirring, until the color changes to a light caramel. Remove immediately, as color will deepen quickly. Do not make caramel until you are ready to dribble over meringues, as the caramel will harden immediately and you will not be able to form a thin stream.

Flan

Preheat oven to 350 degrees
Makes 10 4-ounce cups

2 cups sugar
1 liter milk, scalded (1 quart plus a little more)
4 whole eggs
8 egg yolks
1½ teaspoons vanilla

Beat eggs until foamy. Beat in sugar. Add a little scalded milk to warm the egg mixture to avoid yolks from cooking, then add the rest of the scalded milk. (To scald milk, place milk in a microwaveable container and heat until skin layer appears.)

Add vanilla. Let stand on counter for 2 to 3 hours until foam subsides. Pour into caramelized ramekins or custard cups. Place in baking pan filled with hot water that comes about ⅓ up the sides of the pan.

Bake at 350 degrees for 35 to 40 minutes. Custard is done if you place a knife in the center of flan and it comes out clean.

To serve for breakfast, instead of caramelized cups, spray the ramekins with Pam. Before baking, sprinkle top of custard with a little cinnamon and nutmeg .Custard is a wonderful source of dairy for children. Dessert can be stored for several days in the refrigerator.

To caramelize
1 cup sugar
5 Tablespoons water

In heavy fry pan melt sugar. When mixture becomes clear, boil until color turns a light caramel for two or three minutes. Be careful not to let mixture get to dark, as a burnt taste will result.

Sanibel Ice Cream Turtle Pie

Preheat oven 350 degrees
Serves 6 to 8

1 box graham cracker crust
Melted butter
Vanilla ice cream
Chocolate ice cream
Chocolate fudge sauce
Butterscotch or Caramel sauce
Pecans, chopped and toasted

Follow graham cracker crust recipe on the box, and line a Pam sprayed spring form with prepared crust, making sure the crust is packed into bottom and sides of spring form. Set in freezer for a few minutes to set and then bake at 350 degrees for 5 minutes.

Line cookie sheet or small baking pan with aluminum foil, and spread nuts evenly and top with pats of butter. Bake slowly in 300 degree oven or toaster oven. Watch carefully, as they will burn easily. (10 to 15 minutes or less)

When shell is cooled, fill to ½ with vanilla ice cream, layering cold fudge sauce and cold butterscotch or caramel sauce, as you fill the pie with the vanilla ice cream. Freeze until ice cream is hard.

Stack chocolate ice cream over frozen vanilla, layering the chocolate ice cream with fudge and butterscotch or caramel sauce, as you did with the vanilla. Mound the chocolate ice cream high and top with chopped, toasted nuts.

Freeze. Let pie sit out of freezer for a few minutes before slicing. Cut only what you need, wrap and return left over to freezer.

Note-- any flavor of ice cream may be substituted for vanilla or chocolate. Any flavor ice cream topping may be substituted or added to chocolate and butterscotch or caramel.

Silk Chocolate

Preheat oven to 400 degrees
Serves 8

Crust
½ cup brown sugar
1 cup flour
¼ pound butter
½ cup chopped pecans

In food processor bowl, using the dough or regular blade, combine sugar, flour, and butter. Process until mixture appears like peanut butter. Spread batter on a greased four-sided baking cookie sheet. Spread chopped pecans and bake at 400 degrees for 7 to 8 minutes. To avoid edges from burning, take a fork and stir the batter. Pat back to cookie sheet edge. Return to oven and continue to bake another 8 minutes, or until mixture browns and crumbles. Total baking time for crust is approximately 16 minutes'. Crust may be frozen or stored in the refrigerator.

***Note*--** for English Toffee Bars, cook as above, without nuts. Remove from oven and immediately add Hershey Bars to top. Allow chocolate to melt and sprinkle with chopped nuts. Serve or freeze to store.

Filling
½ pound butter
1½ cups sugar
2 teaspoons vanilla
4 eggs, room temperature
3 squares unsweetened chocolate, melted (3 ounces)

Melt chocolate and butter in microwave and pour into food processor. Add other ingredients. Process until mixture gets very thick .Spread on cool crust...

Topping
2 cups whipped cream, sweetened
Chocolate curls

Top with sweetened whipped cream or cool whip and chocolate curls. Refrigerate. Remove from refrigerator about 30 minutes before serving.

To make as individual desserts, fill bottom of individual greased ramekins with crumble mixture while crumble mixture is hot. Top with chocolate mixture. Freeze or refrigerate. When ready to serve, top with sweetened whipped cream and shaved chocolate. Crust and filling may be made several days ahead and refrigerated or frozen.

Snow Pudding with Custard Sauce

1 Tablespoon (1 package) gelatin
¼ cup cold water
¼ cup fresh squeezed lemon juice
3 egg whites, room temperature, stiffly beaten
1 cup boiling water
1 cup sugar

Soak gelatin in cold water for 5 minutes. Add boiling water, sugar and lemon juice. Stir until dissolved. Strain if necessary. Refrigerate until mixture begins to thicken, but is not as firm as Jell-o. It will be ready when the mixture clings to the sides of the bowl when the bowl is tilted. When mixture begins to thicken, using mixer at low speed, beat in stiffly beaten egg whites. Beat thoroughly. Pour into well greased mold or individual dessert dishes and refrigerate overnight.

To unmold, put hot water in sink and place mold bottom in water for just a very short time. Place serving dish over top of mold and invert. Pudding should come out easily. If not, try loosening sides with a sharp knife before inverting onto platter. An alternate way to unmold is to place a wet towel in the microwave for about 1 minute, on high, and then wrap the towel around the mold. I have always used a plastic mold, where the bottom is removed after the mold is inverted, allowing the mold to release easily without melting

Custard Sauce (see "NAUGHTY SAUCY")

Serve with plenty of custard sauce. It's pretty to pour some of the sauce over the top of the snow mountain and let it cascade down the sides. Serve the remainder of the sauce in a gravy boat. If you are serving the desert in individual dessert dishes, rather than a mold, top with plenty of sauce and serve the remainder of the sauce, on the side. Decorate with strawberries and mandarin oranges (or anything for color).

Strawberry Delight

Serves 10 to 12

Crust
1 box vanilla wafers, crushed
⅓ cup sugar
1 stick butter, melted
1 spring form pan, heavily greased

Melt butter. Crush wafers, using grater attachment on food processor or blender. Add melted butter and sugar, using enough butter to make crust stick to sides of spring form pan. Heavily grease spring form with butter or margarine, not Pam. Pack sides and bottom with crumbs, especially in areas where bottom meets sides. Put in freezer for a few minutes to set.

Filling
1 stick butter
2 eggs, lightly beaten
1 cup sugar
½ to 1 cup chopped pecans

Melt butter in heavy sauce pan. Add sugar and then beaten eggs. Stir constantly over low heat until pudding consistency. Do not burn. Pour over crust. Top with enough pecans to cover. Refrigerate for 1 hour.

Topping
4 cups heavy cream whipped and sweetened with powdered sugar
    to taste
2 quarts strawberries

Wash, dry, and hull strawberries. Slice the little ones, reserving the biggest for the top. Put beater and bowl in freezer before making fresh whipped cream. Whip 4 cups heavy cream.

Layer whipped cream, then sliced strawberries, then whipped cream. Top with the biggest strawberries. Frozen strawberries may be substituted for fresh, but they are not as good.

Note-- desserts can be made individually using custard cups. These can be frozen adding whipped cream and strawberries later. Dream whip or cool whip can be substituted for whipped cream.

Toll House Pie

Preheat oven 325 degrees
Serves 6

1 9 inch unbaked prepared pie shell
2 eggs
½ cups flour
½ cups sugar
½ cups, light brown sugar, packed
½ cups butter, melted and cooled to room temperature
1 cups semi-sweet chocolate chips
1 cups chopped nuts, walnuts or pecans
1 gallon vanilla ice cream, or whipped sweetened whipped cream

In a medium mixing bowl, beat eggs until foamy. Beat in white and brown sugar and flour, until will blended. Blend in melted butter. Stir in chocolate chips and nuts.

Pour into unbaked pie shell. Bake at 325 degrees for 1 hour.

Serve warm and top with ice cream or whipped cream.

Mrs. Brown goes to the Doctor for lab work. Five days later her husband gets a call from the doctor's office, explaining that they had a problem. The nurse explains to Mr. Brown, that they actually had two patients named Brown, with lab work being done at the same time, and the reports got mixed up. Both reports came back with Mrs. Brown's name on it. One lab report, unfortunately, diagnosed Mrs. Brown as having Alzheimer's and the other said that Mrs. Brown was HIV positive. The confused husband asks what he should do? The Doctor's office suggests that he send his wife out for a walk and if she comes back, don't screw her!"

Confessions of a High Priced Caterer
Lettuce help!

Coolers are the best way to keep cooked food warm. Either place a large towel inside your cooler to protect the sides and bottom from the heat, or line your cooler with foil. Wrap cooked food first in plastic wrap and then in foil and place the items inside the lined cooler. If you are only putting a small amount of hot food into a large cooler, add cheap potatoes that have been microwaved on high until cooked. These hot potatoes will give you heat for several hours while you tailgate. This also will allow you to free up your oven for other foods.

Use parchment paper for baking. Baked goods may be wrapped in parchment paper, then in foil and frozen. It is not necessary to unwrap before re-heating.

Curdling can be reversed. When your sauce separates, remove curdled sauce to a cold pan or bowl and place this bowl in a larger bowl filled with ice and a little water. Use an electric emulsifer or electric mixer to whip sauce until it is smooth, thick and not separated. You can also use one or two ice cubes in the curdled mixture and beat until sauce comes back together. When making sauces that can curdle, use a double boiler. Do not allow the water in the bottom pan to simmer as this can cause curdling. Increase heat if sauce does not thicken. Hollandaise and Bérnaise only need to be served at room temperature, because the sauce will go onto food that is already hot. To reheat, allow sauce to reach room temperature. Place a metal cookie in a very hot oven and allow the surface to get hot. Remove pan from oven. Use a rubber spatula to spread a thin layer of sauce over the hot surface. Scape sauce into a gravy boat and serve.

To **whip cream** first freeze beaters and bowl. Make sure cream is very cold, placing it in the freezer for just a few minutes, but do not freeze. An alternative is to place a frozen soft gel pack under your bowl while beating. If cream curdles while whipping, add more cream and continue beating until the whipped cream comes back together. To whip cream well ahead of when you plan to use it, place stiffly beaten mixture in a strainer and place strainer over a larger bowl, in case cream weeps. Refrigerate until ready to use. If you don't have heavy cream on hand, substitute beaten vanilla ice cream.

Powdered sugar can be made by placing granulated sugar in a smoothie machine or powerful blender and pulverized.

Butter that needs to soften quickly will often melt in the microwave. A safer appproach is to use a cheese slicer and create thin butter slices that will soften quickly at room temperature. Clarified butter is used to sauté foods, as butter is likely to burn. If you clarify the butter, you give up the tasty residue. Instead, add 1 tablespoon of olive oil to your unclarified butter, and the butter will not brown. To make garlic butter, push softened butter and garlic cloves through a garlic press. Add chopped leftover fresh herbs and form a log. Roll log in plastic wrap and freeze. Slice off what's needed and return remaining garlic butter to the freezer.

Nuts will increase in flavor if toasted before using in any recipe and will not sink to the bottom of baked goods. Store nuts, toasted or not, in a mason jar and freeze. When chopping nuts in a food processor, reduce sugar in recipe by 2 tablespoons and add the sugar to the nuts to prevent nut butter. Nuts may also be chopped by hand or placed in a strong sealed baggie and pounded. The underneath side may pulverize, so turn bag frequently.

Crème Fraiche is better than sour cream. To make combine 2 tablespoons buttermilk (see Apple Muffins "BREAKFAST IN BED")
2 teaspoons lemon juice and place in a glass bowl cover tightly and let stand at room temperature for 24 hours, or until thickened. It will keep up to a week in the refrigerator.

Prevent molding Cheese by storing cheese in an airtight container with 2 or 3 sugar cubes. They will absorb the moisture and prevent cheese from molding, but replace sugar cubes as they get soggy. Soft cheeses such as goat cheese, are more easily handled if the cheese is frozen slightly before cutting into desired shapes. If you wish to sauté goat cheese shapes, freeze before rolling in unseasoned bread crumbs. Return cheese to freezer until ready to use. Sauté cheese shapes in melted butter until bread crumbs are browned on all sides. Goat cheese will defrost as it cooks but it will not melt.
Use a zester, fork tongs, or vegetable peeler, to grate frozen cheese over salads, when you only need a little. To store a block of feta, create a brine by dissolving 2 teaspoons of salt to a cup of water. Completely submerge cheese in brine, seal and refrigerate. Large blocks of fresh parmesan cheese may be grated in the food processor. To store, wrap small amounts of grated cheese in plastic wrap, place in freezer bags and freeze until ready to use. Use only as much as you need, reseal and refreeze.

Filo, after defrosting, should be sealed in plastic wrap and refrigerated while working with each section. This will keep the edges from getting wet. Work quickly, as sheets dry out. You can't use too much butter.

Gravy can be made ahead of time and frozen to remove fat. If there isn't any time for freezing, wrap ice cubes with cheese cloth and drag through gravy to remove fat.

Mushrooms can be cleaned with paper towels, scooped out with a melon ball and filled using an infant or demitasse spoon, or sliced with an egg slicer. If you choose to wash mushrooms, do not wash more mushrooms than you need at any one time. Refrigerate leftover mushrooms.

To remove outer skin from fruit or tomatoes, drop items into a pot of boiling water for a minute or two, remove, place in a plastic baggie and seal. Steam will be created and skin should rub off easily. Use a vegetable peeler or sharp paring knife to remove any remaining skin. To skin peppers, place directly on stove burner or barbeque grill and blacken all sides. Remove and place blackened peppers in baggie. Seal and let them steam. Remove from bag and using paper towels, rub off blackened skin. Use vegetable peeler or sharp paring knife to remove to remove any remaining skin from peppers.

Soufflé collars are best held together with scotch tape. At Christmas time, crush peppermint candy canes in a sealed baggie and line buttered soufflé dishes with the candy crystals. For individual soufflé dishes, try deep bowls with handles (like onion soup bowls) as they will be easier to remove from the water bath.

Poached eggs are easy to make for a large group. Use a pan with high sides that will fit over 2 stove top burners. Fill part way with water and place coffee cups or mugs in the water bath. Spray cups with Pam and add a pat of butter. When butter melts, add raw egg, salt, pepper and cover. Cook until whites are solid and yokes are soft. To remove egg, run a sharp knife along cup edge and invert.

Tops for pots can be created by completely covering the topless pot with plastic wrap. *Be very careful to prick plastic wrap with the point of a sharp knife away from any part of you or you may get a steam burn.*

Meat can be defrosted quickly by placing the frozen meat in a sealed baggie and submerging the baggie in a bowl of cold water. Do not let water get into the sealed baggie. If baggie floats to the top, weight it down. Cook meat mostly frozen to keep the juices inside. Freeze hamburger in a freezer baggie and flatten meat. When frozen, you can break off what you need. When sautéing, salt the bottom of you skillet instead of oil or butter. This will keep the meat from sticking to the pan while drawing out the fat in the meat. Use a potato masher to break up the meat.

Make Ice Cubes out of left over coffee and tea, so that your drinks won't dilute, especially if making the drinks with hot liquid.

Keep vegetables green by adding a pinch of baking powder to the boiling water.

Pasta water needs oil and salt added to the boiling water. To cook pasta early in the day, drain after cooking but do not rinse. Place pasta in a heavy plastic garbage bag and add olive oil to keep pasta from sticking. Close bag and place in a covered cooler until ready to serve.

Flower filled ice sculpture is great for frozen vodka shooters often served with Bellini's. Empty a large cardboard container of orange juice and rinse. Open cardboard so that all sides are open tall. Place a bottle of vodka in the middle of the empty container and fill ¼ with water. Place small fresh flowers into the water between the vodka bottle and the edge of the cardboard, facing flowers to the outside and freeze until partially set. Repeat until water and flowers have reached the lower edge of the neck of the vodka bottle. Freeze until solid. When ready to use, peel off cardboard and place flower encrusted frozen vodka in a large decorative container filled with ice and arrange shooter glasses along side. Any bottle may be placed in the middle of the cardboard orange juice container and later filled with a candle and used as a centerpiece. Since the ice will melt, make sure you have something underneath the sculpture that is deep enough to accommodate the water.

Opening containers is easy, if you take the pointed end of a beer opener and force it underneath the jar lid. As soon as air gets inside, you will hear the lid pop. To open champagne, use a nut cracker and very slowly twist. The idea is not to pop the cork, as that allows all the bubbles to escape.

Storing onions is best done in a brown paper bag and then refrigerated. To keep eyes from tearing when slicing onions, light a candle (and pray) Wrap celery in plastic wrap and then cover with foil before refrigerating. Strawberries may be stored in cardboard egg containers. Wash and dry before hulling. Use an egg slicer to slice strawberries for perfect slices. Asparagus and fresh herbs should be refrigerated in a container with a little water in the bottom and covered with plastic wrap. To cut asparagus, break off the end of one, where it is tender, then cut the rest of the bunch to that size. Mashed or sliced avocado should be kept around the pit to keep from turning brown. Keep a small spray bottle of lemon juice in your refrigerator to spray on peeled and cut fruit. If you don't want the lemon taste, use a lemon lime soda. Lemon lime soda mixed half and half with water, will also keep a live Christmas tree fresh longer. It also works with certain fresh cut flowers.

High Altitude baking can be tricky. Add ½ cup flour to the recipe in addition to the amount already called for. If you are at 6000 feet or less, soufflés should be successful. If possible, use high powered electric mixer instead of a portable mixer. When folding ingredients, make sure you are incorporating a lot of air into your mixture.

Food processors and their attachments make cooking faster and easier, but electric beaters, blenders, and smoothie machines, may also be used.

Demi glaze can be found at grocers, food specialty shops, or on line. You may substitute beef or chicken consume, however you may find the dish a little saltier. Place frozen demi glaze in a microwavable cup, cover and defrost on high in the microwave. Demi glaze is also available unfrozen in jars.

Measuring shortening, such as Crisco, is easily done by filling a large measuring container with 1 cup of water, then adding shortening until water level now reaches required amount of shortening needed. When measuring sticky ingredients, such as honey, first spray your measuring spoons with Pam or dip them in oil, and the sticky ingredient will easily fall into your bowl.

Molds can be difficult. Tupperware makes plastic molds which can be easily released from the bottom. Other molds need to be heavily sprayed with Pam before filling, and refrigerated until firm. Do not unmold until ready to serve. Place stopper in kitchen sink and fill to about 1/3 with hot water. Run a sharp knife around the inner edges of the mold. Place mold very quickly in the hot water bath, not allowing the water to reach the top of the mold. Remove from hot water bath and invert onto your serving platter.

If you do not hear the mold drop, bang top of the inverted mold with the heavy handle of a knife, until mold releases. If this does not work, repeat the entire process. Molds made with gelatin should not be left in the hot water bath for very long, as they will start to melt and will be a mess to invert and serve. Instead of a hot water bath, try wrapping the mold with a very hot towel, first loosening the edges of the mold with a sharp knife and then inverting the mold onto the serving platter. Do not use a doily on your serving platter.

Dusting with cocoa, instead of flour, can eliminate the white layer that often appears on the bottom of brownies or chocolate layer cakes. To avoid this, dust with cocoa. To cut brownies, use a pizza slicer. If you have frosted your brownies or cakes and wish to make the frosting shiny once again, use a blow dryer on the frosting.

Candles should be kept in the freezer so that they will burn longer.
To make them fit tightly into the candle holder, wrap the candle with foil.

Sweet corn can be easily cooked in the microwave. Shuck the corn and remove all the silk. Place the corn back on top of the tender green inner leaves and place on microwavable platter. Corn may be stacked several layers high. About 12 ears of corn may be cooked at one time. Add about ¼ cup water and 1 Tablespoon of sugar to the corn water. Wrap loosely with plastic wrap, leaving a little corner unsealed. Cook on high for about 12 minutes or until all corn kernels are cooked. Cleaned corn may also be placed in a very large pot of boiling water, sweetened with a little sugar. Cover and turn off heat. Corn will be cooked in a few minutes, but can remain in the water for up to an hour. To remove corn kernels from cooked corn, place corn cob in center of a bundt pan and cut kernels off cob and they will neatly fall into the bottom of the bundt pan.

Dental floss is excellent for cutting cheesecake slices.

Electric knives are wonderful for slicing angel food cake, roast turkey, wraps, and breads.

Individual quiches work well in muffin tins and can easily be removed by loosening edges with a sharp knife and inverting the muffin tins. Individual soufflé dishes or ramekins, also works. You can purchase foil custard cups at a restaurant supply house and make a lot at one time. Freeze and use as needed.

Vegetable peeler is great for cleaning cauliflower, asparagus, and making chocolate curls out of a Hershey bar.

index

Breakfast in Bed	1
Apple Coffee Cake	2
Apple Muffins	3
Belgium Waffles	4
Black Bottom Muffins	5
Carrot Cake and Muffins	6
Carrot Cake Frosting	6
Crepe Batter	7
Éclair Almond Coffee Cake	8
Egg and Sausage Casserole	9
Eggs Benedict	10
Eggs Benedict Ala Roma	10
Elegant Fruit Torte	11
Heart-Healthy Breakfast Casserole	12
Overnight French Toast	13
Sour Cream Coffee Cakes	14
Zucchini Bread	15
Banana Bread	15
Quiche Me	17
Asparagus and Seafood Quiche	18
Basic Quiche Batter	19
Crab Meat Quiche	20
Individual Shrimp Quiches	21
Quiche Lorraine	23
Chile Verde Quiche	29
Smoked Pork and Spinach Pie	24
Naughty Saucy	25
Brown Sauce	26
Bordelaise Sauce	26
Barbeque Sauce for Pork Tenderloin	27
Jack Daniels Barbeque Sauce	27
Stone Crab Mustard Sauce	28
Thousand Island dressing	28
Cocktail Sauce	28
Custard Sauce	29
Crème a Glace	29
Hollandaise Sauce	30
Béarnaise Sauce	30
Mung	30
Grand Marnier Fruit Sauce	31
Sugar Free Chocolate Sauce	32
Newberg Sauce	33
Fricassee Sauce	33
Maitre D' Hotel Butter Sauce	33
Sweet and Sour Sauce	34
Wasabi Aioli	34
Cajun Vodka Sauce	34
Hot Nuts	35
Meringue Pecans	36
Orange Pecans	36
Sweet and Spicy Pecans	37
Toasted Nuts	38
Toasted Almonds	38
Toasted Filberts and Toasted Hazelnuts	38

Skinny Dipping	39
Fanny Farmer	40
New Orleans Dip	40
Cream Cheese Bean Dip	40
Crab Mornay	41
Crab Dip	41
Shrimp Maria	42
Smoked Shrimp & Artichoke Spread	43
Shrimp Dip	43
Taco Bread Round or Salad	44
Spinach Bread Round	44
Soak Me, Stroke Me	45
Marinade for Chicken or Pork	46
Marinade for Steaks	46
Marinade for Tenderloin	46
Foreplay	47
Ahi Tuna	48
Artichoke Appetizer	49
Bellin Crepes	50
Broiled Ham and Almond Stuffed Mushrooms	51
Mushroom Roux	51
Magnificent Mushrooms	52
Bruschetta	53
Chicken Pepperidge Farm Fingers	54
Chicken Teasers	55
Coconut Fried Shrimp	56
Conch Fritters	56
Corn and Black Bean Quesadilla	58
Crispy Shrimp Fried in Wontons	59
Asian Dipping Sauce	59
Elegant Crab	60
Crab in Fluted Filo Cups	60
Fried Lobster	61
Grilled Artichoke	62
Grilled Shrimp in Pea Pods	63
Maryland Crab Cakes	64
Meatballs in Beer	65
Mediterranean Loaf	66
Moroccan Brie Topping	67
Brie with Pino Noir Syrup	67
Mushroom Sherry Toast Cups	68
Cups for Mushroom Sherry	68
Parmesan Shrimp Pillows	69
Pina Colada Shrimp	70
Pita Triangles	70
Salmon Topped Potato Pancake with Caviar	71
Shrimp Log	72
Spanakopetes	73
Greek Cheese Pies	74
Stuffed Red Skin Potatoes	75
Crab Chantilly Cream	76
Surf and Turf Tenderloin Teasers	77
Zucchini Tidbits	78

index

Lettuce Dress You	79
Asparagus Salad	80
French Salad Dressing	80
Balsamic Dressing	81
Balsamic Vinaigrette Dressing	81
Bruschetta Seashell Pasta Salad	82
Chicken Endive & Roquefort Salad	83
Mustard Vinaigrette Dressing	83
Chicken Spiral Pasta Salad	84
Cobb Salad with Blue Cheese Dressing	85
Blue Cheese Dressing	85
Deviled Egg Salad	86
Exotic Chicken Salad	87
Tarragon Chicken Salad	87
Flaming Hot Spinach Salad	88
Vinaigrette Dressing	88
French Silk Potato Salad to Die For	89
Fresh Broccoli Mandarin Salad	90
Sweet and Sour Hollandaise Dressing	90
Granny Smith Salad with Balsamic Dressing	91
Baby Blue Salad	91
Greek Orzo Salad	92
Vinaigrette	92
Greek Pasta Salad	93
Greek Vinaigrette	93
Sour Cream Dressing	93
Greek Pasta Dressing	94
Heirloom Tomato Salad	95
Colorful Tomatoes	95
Shrimp and Avocado Salad	96
Shrimp and Mandarin Salad	97
Mandarin Salad Dressing	97
Spicy Peanut Pasta Salad	98
Ginger Vinaigrette Dressing	99
Spinach Daisy Salad	100
Spinach Salad Dressing	100
Strawberry Banana Jell-O Mold	101
Raspberry Jell-O Mold	101
Strawberry – Spinach Salad	102
Strawberry Spinach Salad Dressing	102
Raspberry Pear Spinach Salad	103
Raspberry Salad Dressing	103
Summer Salad	104
Summer Salad Dressing	104
Tahoe Salad	105
Wild Rice & Crab Salad	106
Nooners	107
California Roll Ups	108
Crock Pot Cheese Soup	109
Leek and Potato Soup	109
Five Onion Soup	110
Baked Onion Soup	111
Gazpacho Soup	112
Low Fat Cold Zucchini Soup	112
Hamburgers Sunnyside Up	113
Lump Crab filled Avocado	114
Sandwiches	115
Wraps	116
A Fare to Remember	123
Wild Chicks	119
Amazing Chicken Cacciatore	120
Chicken Crepes	121
Chicken Jubilee	123
Chicken Marsala	124
Chicken Mozzarella	125
Chicken Picatta	126
Coq Au Vin (Chicken in Red Wine)	127
Fried Chicken – Italian Style	128
Poached Chicken	129
Roast Turkey - Old Fashioned Way	130
Gravy	130
Spanish Chicken with Apricots	132
Stir-Fried Almond Chicken	133
Oriental Walnut Chicken	134
In the Boeuf	135
Chili with Filo	136
New York Sweet Chili	137
Day Ahead Classic Brisket	138
Do Ahead Roast Beef	139
Frozen Boneless Rib Roast	139
Grilled Sirloin Steak	140
Individual Beef Wellington	141
Tenderloin of Beef	143
Hook it and Cook it	145
Artichokes Stuffed with Shrimp	146
Barbequed Shrimp	147
Crab Defusky	148
Lobster with Mushroom Buerre Blanc	149
Mushroom Buerre Blanc	149
Paella	150
Shrimp Creole	151
Shrimp Scampi	152
Snapper Fillet with Crabmeat Oscar	153
Grilled Salmon with Pistachio Pesto	154
Grilled Teriyaki Salmon with Sesame Pea Pods	154
Ménage à Trois	154
Baby Rack of Lamb	156
Grilled Lamb Chops	158
Grilled Pork Chops	158
Grilled Pork Tenderloin	158
Grilled Veal Chops	159
Pork Chops with Roasted Garlic Cranberry Bordelaise	160
Bordelaise Sauce	160
Veal Chops with Mushrooms	161
Gravy	161
Veal Scaloppini Marsala	162
Veal Foyot	163

index

Barbequed Lemon Duckling	164
Lotsapastabilities	**165**
Pasta Alfredo	166
Bucatini	166
Easy Penne Pasta with Tomato Cream Vodka Sauce	167
Linguini with Clams and Shrimp	168
A Little Something on the Side	**169**
Apple Stuffing	170
Apples with Jack	170
Cheesy Crusted Cauliflower	171
Tomato, Broccoli Cauliflower Baskets	169
Cheesy Potatoes	172
Chili Rellano	173
Coconut Sweet Potato Casserole	174
Marshmallow Sweet Potatoes	174
Corn Casserole	175
Fiesta Corn	175
Fried Rice with Barbequed Pork	176
Barbequed Pork	176
Garlic Broccoli Florets with Cashews	177
Sesame Asparagus	177
Beer Fritter Cover Batter	178
Beer Batter	178
Make Day Ahead Cheese Soufflé	179
Rough Mashed Red Skin Potatoes	180
Roasted Red Skins	180
Garlic Roasted Potatoes	180
Southern Sweet Potato Pie	181
Spinach Noodle Ring	182
Spinach with White Raisins	183
Easy Creamed Spinach	183
Sweet Potato Pancakes with Citrus and Cranberry Relish	184
Combination Pancakes	185
Heavenly Potato Pancakes	185
Whipped Carrots in Orange Cups	186
Frenched String Beans or Petite String Beans	186
Afternoon Delight	**187**
Non-Alcoholic Toddy	188
Homemade Irish Cream	188
Chocolate Raspberry Saddle Shoes	188
Cocoquito	189
Egg Nog	189
Paradise Found	190
Punch For All Occasions	190
Park Avenue Punch	190
White Punch	190
The Perfect Frozen Margarita	191
The Big Orange	191
Mocha Brandy Frozen Drink Dessert	192
Let's See Some Cheesecake	**193**
Best Cheesecake Ever	194
Differently Delicious Cheesecake	195
Little Bites Cheesecakes	196
Sour Cream Filling	196
New York Cheesecake	197
Ricotta Cheesecake	199
Secret Cheesecake Recipe	200
Yummy Nummies	**201**
Brownies - Regular or Mint	202
Velvety Brownie Icing	202
Chocolate Chewies	203
Ginger Creams	204
Current Jelly Gems	204
Hello Dollies	205
Peanut Butter Chocolate Drops	206
Pecan Puffs	207
Pecan Tassels	208
Happy Endings	**209**
Boûche de Noël	210
Good Mocha Icing	211
Bread Pudding	212
Custard Sauce	210
Butterscotch Bread Pudding	213
Bread Pudding Whiskey Sauce	213
Brownie Ice Cream Sandwich	214
Angel Food Cake with Caramel Frosting	215
Caramel frosting	215
Chocolate Bavarian Pie	216
Chocolate Chip Cake	217
Chocolate Soufflé	218
White Sauce	218
Ice Cream Sauce	219
Crème Brûlée	220
Dessert Crepe	221
Apple Crepes	221
Strawberry Filled Crepes	221
Banana Crepes	221
Chocolate Crepes	222
Floating Island with Caramel Drizzle	223
Flan	224
Sanibel Ice Cream Turtle Pie	225
Silk Chocolate	226
Snow Pudding with Custard Sauce	227
Strawberry Delight	228
Toll House Pie	229

Acknowledgements

"LETTUCE US MAKE YOU LAUGH" has been a labor of love, made possible by all my family and dear friends. You all know how much I love you and appreciate all your time end efforts. To all my wonderful family, who have always been my best food critics. To Sherry, who created Miss Lettuce. To Nancy, for hours of formating and to Pete for putting up with it. To Verena, Kate, and Helen for all the typing. Sincere thanks goes to Michael, Janet, Barbara, John, Katie, David, Lindsay and Kirsten, for all their computer help, since I was hopeless. To Trudy for helping to find lost recipes and for putting up with me for all these years! To Jackie, Shyla, Kathy and Trudy for proof reading. To John, for art consultaion and to Gary for the graphics. To all my friends, for their wonderful recipes, jokes, and continuous encouragement. And to my Mom, who always wanted to write a cookbook. All recipes and jokes in this book have been in my family for years, contributed by friends, or are my own creations.

About the Author - Jill Lundberg

Jill is a 70 year old retired caterer, University of Michigan graduate, married fifty years, mother of three, grandmother of nine. In 1991, she and her daughter-in-law, Trudy, owned and operated Gourmet to Go, Party Planners, Inc., a catering company, successfully serving the greater Orlando area for sixteen years. Their catering events included corporate functions, weddings, special events, and private parties. The company catered events for as many as 1300 AT&T employees, but their most memorable event was at the Cape Canaveral Planetarium, where four hundred and fifty guests of Astronaut Domm Gorie heard him give a very emotional speech directly to us from the space capsule, just prior to his blast off. There wasn't a dry eye, as we all wished him God Speed on his mission.

Gourmet to Go, Party Planners, Inc., retired, when Trudy and her family relocated to the Denver area. Jill, a silver life master, teaches bridge to gifted classes 1st through 5th grades, at Bear Lake Elementary School, Altamonte, Florida. Her young students have won Junior National Events and placed 9th overall in Junior North American School bridge tournament. She is also an avid golfer, knitter and reader. Creating new recipes and wowing her family and friends with new and delicious tastes, still remains her passion.

About the Illustrator - Sherri Ratsma

A love of the Arts has always been inside of me. As a child I drew all the time, as I was a farmers daughter in the country in Michigan, and with no brothers or sisters, I got quite good, I just never did anything with my abilities until my four children were grown and gone. I picked up the paint brush and began at the age of 50. Since that time, and with only one class in oils, I began to win award after award. Most all my paintings are portraits,and some Landscapes. This is my first cartoon art, Miss Lettuce Head.

Contact Us

Feel free to contact us at: **lettucehelps@gmail.com**.
To order additional books, please go to **www.amazon.com**.

Made in the USA
Charleston, SC
23 February 2014